Casebook for Christian Living

CASEBOOK FOR CHRISTIAN LIVING

*Value formation for families
and congregations*

**ROBERT A. and ALICE F. EVANS
and
LOUIS and CAROLYN WEEKS**

John Knox Press
ATLANTA

Library of Congress Cataloging in Publication Data

Main entry under title:

Casebook for Christian living.

   Includes bibliographical references.
   1. Christian life—Presbyterian authors.
I. Evans, Robert A., 1937–
BV4501.2.C337   248'.48'51   77–79587
ISBN 0–8042–2032–8

10 9 8 7 6 5 4 3

Contents

75814

Introduction

Presented here are twelve cases. Each of these cases records an actual experience, although each has a superficial disguise to prevent embarrassment or misunderstanding as well as to protect the privacy of those who shared their experiences. Participants in the situations have provided releases of the cases as essentially correct versions of the events and transactions as they perceived them.

Each case offers a crisis or problem which demands a decision. Note that while we may not encounter every one of these problems in our own lives, we all face issues and dilemmas similar to these. Our decisions usually involve less dramatic situations, but the values and models we bring to bear are the same for all conditions. How shall we behave in the midst of life experiences? Studies have shown that we cannot program or predict our reaction to people or events. But we can as Christians draw on the resources of our faith community and our religious commitment to understand the implications of our decisions and the values which guide them. How do we go about that process together?

The twelve cases are organized by the areas of life in which decision-making and modeling may focus: (1) Family, (2) Church, (3) Society, and (4) the universal issues of Life, Sustenance, and Death. These cases are accompanied by study guides, a drawing together of possible themes and avenues of discussion. Each guide suggests ways of using the cases to explore guidelines for Christian living. The principal values on which the four sections focus are (1) Loving, (2) Trusting, (3) Responding, and (4) Hoping. It is important to note that the twelve study guides differ in detail and suggested approaches. The longer guides for the first cases offer more specific suggestions to the reader new to case discussion. The study guides also offer numerous approaches to style and content of group discussion. The authors hope you will adapt the different techniques to your own style.

The cases are preceded by brief introductory essays, guides for Christian living, which are concerned with our understanding of Christian life. These essays consider how congregations can function effectively as an extended family and how the study of cases among members of a congregation might aid in corporate and individual Christian growth and parish revitalization. It is not necessary to read all the essays before diving into the cases and the exciting discussions which tend to occur. We hope that our interpretations and suggestions will not stand in your way, but trust that you will use what is helpful among these resources.

Three goals of congregational life suggested here are wisdom, maturity, and discernment. Our personal experience gives evidence that the case method approach contributes to the fulfillment of these aims. We first seek to integrate insights from the Bible and church traditions with the ideas and experiences of families and congregations while we suggest the helpfulness of cases as vehicles for actively incorporating those insights into our own value systems. Second, we offer some hints in facilitating discussions and preparing to teach and learn from cases. Third, as we present the cases with the study guides, we focus on your ability and insight in Christian decision-making and living. We will have more to say about these goals of congregational life, the meaning of "case," value modeling, and revitalization of parish life in the introductory essays.

It is crucial to declare that neither the discussion of Christian values nor the study guides pretends to give the Christian solution to any single problem posed in the cases. In our judgment there is no *one* answer provided by the Christian gospel for each human dilemma exposed in the cases. Rather, there is a range of faithful and loving Christian responses. The case method trusts in the resources of the teacher and his or her material, but it trusts even more in the resources of the participants and of the congregations. The case method encourages and facilitates dialogue so that the wisdom of alternatives may emerge in the community. However, we are not suggesting ethics by consensus. The ultimate trust is in God who by the Spirit gives us the freedom to respond, the grace to decide, and even the forgiveness to be wrong.

One goal of this project is that each participant will recognize and celebrate his or her role as a theologian—one who thinks about the reality of human life in the world from the perspective of Christian faith in God. The Bible and theology are resources that inform our perspective and decision-making. The teacher or student may also want to check with reflections from past communities of faith. Each study guide includes one or two references to books or articles that allow us to see how other communities, including the biblical community, have reflected on the issues. Most of these come from a biblical or theological perspective, but some are recommended to provide additional information on a subject or to reflect cultural values. Remember, however, that the suggested books and study guides are never a substitute for your own reflection; they are only an aid for clarification and focus. If we were to suggest any one connecting thread in your exploration for alternatives as you study the cases, this would be in the simple question, "What is the most loving thing to do at this time?" The family and the congregation are resources for responding to that question. We call you to trust and hope in the resources of one another as gifts of Christ's grace.

We need to thank colleagues and companions in the Christian pilgrimage. Keith Bridston and Jerry Handspicker, leaders in the Case-Study Institute which seeks to enrich theological education through use of cases, have been particularly important and we appreciate their contributions. Other seminary faculty members throughout North America, more than a hundred of them, have shared in the exploration of case writing and case teaching and we are grateful for their efforts.

To the staff and instructors of the C.S.I. summer workshops (1972–77) and to the staff of the Association of Theological Schools, particularly Jesse Ziegler, the Executive Director, we express our debt of gratitude for dialogue, critique, and support.

This casebook is dedicated to those members of the Christian family who have shared their experiences and to the congregations who shared their insights, enabling others to grow in the art of Christian living.

PART I
Guidelines
for Christian Living

1 / Values, Modeling, and the Christian Community

What Is Christian Living?

"I came that they might have life, and have it abundantly."—John 10:10

"You are the family of Christ." The whole congregation listened, but the children gathered at the front of the sanctuary seemed most intent. The minister continued: "Now I want you to help me as we take in another family member. Will you pretend somebody knocked on the door and go answer it? Welcome them to our family!"

The children jostled to the side door, opened it, and said "Come on in" to the mother, father, and baby waiting there. After everyone surrounded the baptismal font, the minister proceeded with the sacrament. "Here is Donald Matthew. May I have him to introduce him to the rest of the family, at least to the ones here this morning?" The minister took Donald Matthew in his arms. He walked up and down the aisle, and then back to the children and to Donald's parents up front. After prayer, he said: "Donald Matthew, child of the covenant, I baptize you in the name of the Father, the Son, and the Holy Ghost." A child held the bowl of water, while the minister used it to baptize the baby. "Let's remember as we receive Donald Matthew into our family, we accept responsibility for his growing in Christ. We also think about our growing together in Christian life."

Susan and Jim Ross exchanged a wink as they sat quietly watching the baptism and thinking about their own children in similar times. Todd, their active eight-year-old, trouped proudly back to the pew. Passing by his fifteen-year-old sister, Carol, he stepped on her toe. "Stop it, Todd." Here was the Ross family, in the middle of their larger, extended family of the congregation.

It hadn't been an easy year for the Rosses. Not by any means. Jim had lost his job in the company cutback, the Rosses had moved here. Things were particularly difficult for Carol, a sophomore leaving lots of friends at the wrong time. In the new situation, there had been tension about making new acquaintances, dating patterns for Carol, and a proper school for Todd. To top it all off, Grandpa Ross had been seriously ill and medical decisions were difficult by long distance and necessitated trips back and forth. Prayer—though it was sometimes hard to know what to pray for—had been an important resource for the family this year.

Yet here they sat, reminded again of the image of the church as a great, extended family of Christ. They had found brothers and sisters—even aunts, uncles and cousins—among the members of this congregation. And as they understood it, they shared this family life with Christians all over the world. They were participating in a rich new existence in a new place and beginning to experience that abundant life, promised in the faith, the promise of Christian life.

The Ross family had become members of this congregation soon after they chanced on it, the second church they had visited on their self-confessed "shopping tour" after arrival in town. Jim had said it for all of them: "I felt at home almost immediately. There was an honest sense of acceptance. The members of the church not only accept but expect things of us." The Rosses felt the emphasis was on the quality of relationships between people more than on programs.

It was becoming clear to the Rosses more than ever that some values and commitments characterized Christian living. The classic biblical emphasis on faith, hope, and love seemed to find definite expression. Church school treated them like a family. A parish group combined support with loving critique that enabled them to grow. For Carol the key lay in senior fellowship, which focused on the real problems and issues for teenagers, such as curfew times. According to Jim, the most helpful times were discussions in a series on "Death and Life from a Christian Perspective." Susan had been asked to help out in an adult education program that used cases, a method of teaching new to her. She recognized a new self-awareness and self-confidence in her abilities and thoughts.

Susan and Jim were clear that there was still a lot of "settling in" to be done in their family; there would be other crises. They were sure the "abundant life" never intended to exclude struggle or pain. But they had found values and models for coping, even growing, in a year of turmoil. The witness and support of their new extended family had been instrumental in the process.

For other families within this family of Christ the same kinds of things were taking place. Nobody appeared to live "above it all." Even in the "family squabbles" among members, sometimes with the energetic but disorganized pastor, most people undergirded their differences with mutual respect. The Rosses had discovered it went beyond superficial friendliness which could cover up problems and issues. Members "hung in there" to help out with the children when Jim and Susan needed to visit Grandpa Ross. Here lived a real extended family, a Christian community, alive and deeply linked to the world in the name of Jesus Christ.

Impossible? Not in the experience of the authors. We have found some examples of really vital Christian living, of exceedingly healthy churches, and we delight in the prospect of more. In the study of an organic community, and invitations to share its growth, we begin with a look at Christian values.

Christian Values

"Do not neglect to do good and to share what you have . . ."—Hebrews 13:16

What are your values? What is important in your life? Doing good? Sharing? Being honest? Loving justice? Peace? Mercy? Faith?

Now consider the ways in which you came to prize those values. Were your parents a major example for you? Friends? Teachers? The probability is great that many of your cherished values have been transmitted (that means "handed-over") to you in part by members of your extended family. On the other hand you have been, and continue to be, exercising some choice in the formation of your value structure. Among conflicting values you are constantly choosing, and hopefully you are growing in the process.

Can values be learned? A debate among social scientists now centers on this topic, as on the attendant one: "If values are learned, how does this process take place?" Some argue that values are really determined by heredity, or by circumstances over which one has no control. Others consider change and growth not only possible, but even begin to offer ways of getting at that re-orientation of people in living situations.

Perhaps we cannot resolve once for all that conflict, but we can focus on clear, accepted Christian values among ourselves. We can encourage each other, as well as the children in our "family," to increase in sensitivity and grow morally. Take this clear word from the writer of Hebrews, for example: "Do not neglect to do good and to share what you have." Or consider the classic statement of the chief virtues by Paul in 1 Corinthians 13:13: "So faith, hope, love abide, these three; but the greatest of these is love." In these instances and many others, we have clear statements of Christian values. How do we incorporate these values, and others we can name easily, in our living? What about the inconsistencies and the need for growth?

To supply just one illustration, at a recent session with adults in a church school one man spoke of his situation with some dismay: "Something's wrong! When people ask me about it, I tell them how much I love my family and how important they are in my life. But when I figure how I spend my time, I find I don't act as though they were so important at all. My energies go elsewhere." His group of church school colleagues had been discussing the case of a family breaking up. Members of the group could have greeted this man's self-revelation in a variety of ways. They could have ignored him, scoffed at him, or scolded him. Instead they listened, and one person signaled hearing him: "The priorities seem mixed up. . . ." Conversation moved along with the man still included in it. And, subsequently, he began to act more the caring parent and spouse.

The church group, in this situation, seems both to have helped the man clarify his present enacted values and move toward the formation of values he would move to act upon. What is true for a Christian person is also true for a Christian community. Its values often need to be clarified, but they are also formed within the church. There are numerous guides on "value clarification" available for use in schools and churches. Through growing in the faith, Christian families at the nuclear and congregational levels can come to develop and act on Christian values as well as clarifying present commitments.

All too often, however, the families in which we participate are abdicating responsibility for the valuing process. At the same time social forces—mobility and haste in American life, dehumanizing movie and television programming, role confusions, racial tension on a world wide basis, and family separations on a large scale—are occupying a center stage today unparalleled in human history.

The church is not now aiding in value formation as it used to. In the words of Louis Raths and Sidney Simon, two moral educators, "In the early years of the century the church . . . seemed to have a greater influence . . . than it does today." These remarks were focused on the valuing process for children, but they apply to all of us. According to these men, "There was a gradual but continuing separation of family life from frequent church and Sunday school participation. This meant a decrease in the quantity and quality of contact with religious traditions and their emphasis upon values."

It is unrealistic to expect immediate change in the cultural situation of all persons. But we can center consciously on supporting and encouraging Christian patterns of living that prize and seek to embody central values in our tradition—love for others, for instance. We must discover methods to understand better what the Christian idea of love requires of us in situations of conflict and decision.

We can likewise seek to live in a consciously Christian manner ourselves, learning from other believers and from people we trust the ways in which to cope and creatively deal with our daily commitments and possibilities. Discussions of values in

Bible study, in peer groups, with families and friends, can help clarify and even form (sometimes "re-form") the values on which we seek to depend.

Modeling as a Process

"I am reminded of your sincere faith, a faith
that dwelt first in your grandmother Lois
and your mother Eunice and now, I am sure,
dwells in you."—2 Timothy 1:5

Children and grownups, too, follow examples in forming their values and acting upon them. We do it consciously, and we do it unconsciously as well. Sometimes the early learnings are so obvious in modeling they make us laugh. Not long ago some friends came to the house to visit. Their child was a toddler, younger than our own kids. He clung at first to his parents' clothes, peeked from behind them, remained cautious in a new place. But his eyes followed every move our children made. He began to venture to their toys—cars and trucks—after a while. Then our boy, sensing the change in Bryan, the young visitor, stooped to run a race car across the floor. "Vrrrooommm!" he went as he did it. Bryan walked straight to the car, took it is his hand, said, "Vrrrooommm!" and sped it across the floor in precisely the same manner the older boy had done. All of us grownups, watching the sequence of events, praised Bryan for his new activity. (Relief! He was beginning to enjoy himself, and let us visit, too.)

Off Bryan went, following the older kids, copying, and now sticking to them like glue. Every once in awhile, he would check our reaction. We would all say, "Good."

Now all of us at times notice ourselves doing the same kinds of things as Bryan. We imitate people with apparent power and winsomeness. Sometimes this influence on us is negative, as cultural or peer pressures move us to lesser values and superficial living. But the process of modeling can also lead us into maturity and growth.

Christian discipleship has traditionally focused us on this

process in the faith. Jesus called disciples himself, and he told believers to "follow" him. Paul, and the other New Testament writers, emphasize Christians modeling religious experience and ways of living. It is impossible to be a Christian alone. Our growth is affected by others since we are "members one of another" in the body of Christ, the Church. Corporately, we model the life of the early church. For each and all of us, modeling is a natural and crucial way of being in the world as Christians. We even "check out" our behavior (like Bryan did) as we share, pray, meditate, and worship. We seek gifts of forgiveness, growth, care, and other reinforcements from God through our brothers and sisters in Christ.

We recognize the importance of values, and we know that we follow models in forming them and in choosing among them. How do we support each other in this modeling, in this forming of value structures that sustain real Christian living? How shall we learn from each other and receive encouragement for ethical behavior, mature choices, and wise restraint? Logically, the best way of maintaining the system of support among us is for all of us to follow each other through experiences. We could then share the questions and resources, the ideas and the rewards of growth. The image that comes to mind is of a medical intern, surrounded by supervisors and trusted peers, giving treatment that represents their corporate wisdom while the intern learns in the process. At first the medical student watched, then she imitated the behavior of others, and now she is acting while others watch and help.

This may be a good image, but we cannot possibly sustain the pattern in actual living. Our lives and society are much too complex. Following the modeling process, how can we gain the extra insight and assistance in living the Christian life—more than what we already receive in the tacit program of modeling, the one we use now? We gather as a worshiping and working congregation. In good times we elicit joy and satisfaction as a community; we also "share each others' woes, our mutual burdens bear. . . ."

If we focus consciously on what we are doing, however, we can augment the efforts. We can instruct ourselves, take up our responsibility for mutual growth, and concentrate on developing a pattern for Christian living. This is the pattern we perceive in one especially powerful model, the life in the early Christian community. Paul was willing, even eager, to call the attention of the community to high values as he sought to model living by them: "The fruit of the Spirit is love, joy, peace, patience, kindness, goodness, faithfulness, gentleness, self-control." (Galatians 5: 22–23).

As Paul sought to model, he tried to follow the family patterns and those values embodied in the members. But he especially tried to follow the model of Jesus, the one in whose name the family lives. Since new problems were always being faced by individual Christians and the Christian community, Jesus' words and actions as a wise, mature, and discerning model had to be interpreted and applied. It was the community of loyalty and interpretation that helped apply the implications of the model to a new situation. It was Jesus as the head of a living and maturing body which was the image behind mutual respect and mutual responsibility for each member and organ of that body. The "extended family" of Christ is an interpretation of the "body of Christ."

Christian Living in the Early Church

"The whole body of believers were united in heart and soul. . . . They had never a needy person among them. . . ."—Acts 4:32, 34 N.E.B.

What is so attractive and authoritative about that early Christian "family"? Why does it have so much power for us? For one thing, the early church had a continuity with the life, death, and resurrection of Jesus himself. If the gospels tell what Jesus was like and what he did, the Acts of the Apostles tells what Jesus' body, or "family," was like and what Jesus continued to do in the world as Christians lived in it. The narrative of Acts is similar to the Gospel according to Luke, with scarcely a break at all in the story.

For another thing, the early church was clearly the recipient of God's Spirit. The events of Pentecost and the "gifts of the Spirit" remain at the core of the account. By the Spirit's power people believed and hoped, leaders led, Stephen remained courageous, Peter preached, and Paul evangelized. By the power of God's Spirit the world began to change and Christian worship formed its traditions. Some people have interpreted the crucial part of this process to have been a particular portion of the family's life together (their speaking in tongues, their communal sharing, their religious assemblies, and so forth). Yet the pattern of life, the whole of the fabric, seems more important than any single element. The model is grounded in ways in which these early Christians responded in grace and in judgment to the situations that confronted them.

We see this family united, in the words of Luke, "in heart and soul." Here is an incredibly attractive picture of a group of persons who share and respond to one another's burdens continually and concretely. The text goes so far as to declare that "they never had a needy person among them." We recall that "need" in the early church was defined as much in terms of loneliness, anxiety, and frustration as in terms of hunger. These Christians experienced "table fellowship" as they ate, shared, witnessed, served, and sang songs.

Christian living as portrayed in the New Testament acquired a beat, a rhythm, which even in the midst of all the various events had some common elements: They prayed together, they cared for one another, they believed together in the power of Christ, and they all expected the coming kingdom. They lived in love, faith, and hope.

That family of Christ came to depend on the transforming presence of Jesus' Spirit to bind them together even in the midst of disagreements and conflicts. We find that they did not create this sense of community by themselves. Rather, they celebrated it as a gift of God. And we learn daily that all these gifts of faith, hope, love, and the rest come not from ourselves. They are from God.

Christians through the ages have been drawn to the image of the early church in their quest for Christian authenticity and life. God has granted renewal in a variety of persons, movements, and institutions. Look for example, at the monastic movement which has provided new life for the church in many ways through the centuries. The monks sought from the first, probably in the third century in Egyptian churches, to follow the examples of Jesus, Peter, and Paul, among others. They were descendants of Stephen the Martyr in their commitment. They sought to obey the commands of Jesus to the young ruler (Luke 18:22), and of Paul to the Corinthians (1 Corinthians 7:7, 30). The friars in the Church sought not monastic isolation from the world but a family "of brothers" from which they could better serve the needs of the world. It is the quality of relationship in a life together that was renewed in this model. Support and critique in community was seen as essential for Christian living. So in religious communities both monks and friars have sought to inherit the gifts given the early community.

The sixteenth century reformers—Luther, Calvin, and John Knox among them—sought to re-instate the authority and vitality of that "first family" for people in their changing world. The leadership of the pastoral and sacramental life we Protestants know has been patterned directly on the interpretation of the early church life as reformers understood it in their reading of Scripture. It was the mutual ministry and service under the image of the "priesthood of all believers" that restored the communal concern of the church in Acts. Although different reformers may have thought they recaptured the essence of the early church, they are seen to have brought much of their own personalities and traditions into the churches in their own day.

Institutions—and the family and church are indeed institutions—are organic in nature. Congregations or communions cannot just leapfrog the intervening centuries and move Christians again into the first century. We can, however, rely on God's gifts as did the early Christians. We can care for each other, for people in the world, and for the world itself. We can believe in chorus with the early community in the power of God, in the work of Christ. And we can hope for "God's will on earth as in heaven." This early Christian community can be a model, and their values can become our's. We look for the time when we might again confess about the family of Christ, "The whole body of believers were united in heart and soul."

Parish Revitalization

"And he who sat upon the throne said, 'Behold, I make all things new.' "—Revelation 21:5

The quest for "parish revitalization" has become a concern, almost an obsession, for some congregations in recent years. The programs have to be "new" ones, the educational materials "innovative," and the leadership "fresh." A portion of this quest is truly valid, for congregations as individuals tend at times to become "set in our ways." But many congregations seek not only criteria for re-vitalization; they also seek specific means of achieving this goal as though there existed a single pattern from which to attain newness and life. Some people have even tended to use a kind of shopping list, supposing that if all the products were bought and mixed just so—Presto, chango! Revitalization! We are tempted, like Simon the Magician (Acts 8:9–24), to want to conjure God's power of life on our terms.

As the early Christian congregations discovered, however, we cannot pattern ourselves and our gifts uniformly to one set of external criteria for newness and life. Research by educators indicates that people learn in quite different ways, at differing rates. Congregations, too, respond and grow in a variety of ways. Perhaps an appropriate inquiry is not so much for a set of criteria as for images and symbols of vital interaction among members of the community of faith and those they seek to serve. We have the models of early church life, distinctive in the various places where Christians gathered and lived. We see the values they shared and the many ways in which they embodied those values in vital ministering and worship. Discerning a rhythm for the family's Christian life may be possible, but it has to occur in the community itself. Nobody can impose it from outside. Rather than the superficial product of a gimmick or new technique, this rhythm must have the sustaining power based in a capacity for spiritual depth.

One biblical image of life is the very term for Holy Spirit used in the Scriptures: "breath." The Holy Spirit is the breath of God, breathing life into the body of Christ. To be sustained and to live abundantly, both human and congregational (family) life require a natural rhythm of breathing to energize the organism. Spiritual and physical breath are both indispensible for survival. Yet the gift of the Spirit is found and exists among persons and congregations in different ways. Encounters with God's Spirit have a variety of manifestations and consequences, as the New Testament and our own experiences illustrate.

A variety of methods and processes can assist in "vitalizing" congregational life, (or "re-vitalizing" it, with parishes that formerly were lively). But "re-vitalization" does not mean a return to a former time when a congregation felt alive. Just as we cannot recapture the lifestyle of the early church, we cannot revitalize primarily by turning back the pages of history. The term rather suggests the recovery of an image or model of a congregation, a Christian family, filled with abundant life.

While there can be no outside pattern to determine whether a congregation is vital, or how to revitalize it, we can glimpse the quality of relationships and the Christian values alive in our midst. Particular histories, some patterns of congregational life, and certain new methods may nurture vitalization more than others, yet only the Spirit can guarantee the breath of life. At least for some of us, certain characteristics of a vital congregation seem to be generally present. These find a variety of expressions, and even different vocabularies are used by the families to talk about them:

(1) *Faith.* Does the community look to God, not just to itself, for resources and abundance in life? (Is the family repentant?) Is the sinfulness, the tendency for making errors and shallow commitments, acknowledged? Does forgiveness accompany accountability and confession?

(2) *Integrity.* Do the members speak "the truth in love," are they free to say "Yes," "No," and whatever is true in between concerning times of interdependence and those of independence? (Is the family honest?) Can mutual critique be expressed without rancor, and mutual support without embarrassment?

(3) *Growth.* Do the members grow from being with each other, and do they feel free to learn as well as to teach? (Is the family educational?) Do encounters with other family members allow one to be freer, more fulfilled, and more joyful?

(4) *Responsibility.* Are the needs of the world acknowledged and are the members striving to meet those needs individually and institutionally? (Is the family ethical?) Is a family-in-mission a priority?

(5) *Openness.* Does the life and work, the worship and play of the congregation focus on the world and the church in the whole world? (Is the family ecumenical?) Is the family open to hear the Spirit's presence in the recommendations and judgments of God's children in other churches and outside the church?

(6) *Hope.* As people lead in worship and work, do the members expect the Spirit of God to be in their midst, interpreting and luring them forward toward God's promised kingdom? (Is the family expectant?) Do they genuinely expect and anticipate that their life together will be made new?

To say it one more time, these and other questions cannot become a recipe of some sort imposed from the outside. They are guidelines for discovering a rhythm of life together. The pattern may be discerned as each family listens and has dialogue with other, more distant relatives. But the vitality, the newness and refreshment are God's gifts which come to us from within the spirit and distinctiveness of the congregation—from its own talents and needs, mission, and style. It is Christ who makes "all things new" as he lives in us and between us.

Goals of Congregational Life

"A disciple is not above his teacher, but every one when he is fully taught will be like his teacher."—Luke 6:40

Christian living in and through the extended family of Christ has goals, as well as characteristic qualities. The goals of wisdom, maturity, and discernment are among the ends toward which a Christian community strives. The Middle English word from which "goal" comes means "boundary." The boundaries of human existence, the widest goals toward which people strive, suggest an image of "moving out" from a confining center. The notion of "boundary" also implies that these goals are of such magnitude that they will never be completely attained. Yet they remain objectives that influence the rhythm of communal life and establish expectations of interaction.

Note that we are identifying goals for congregations first, and only secondarily are we suggesting these as goals for the individual Christian. These are values that do not emerge when we are alone. They develop and are tested only in relation to others. Wisdom, maturity, and discernment are representative goals for congregational life more than they are comprehensive goals. They are gifts of the Spirit which usually come through ones presence in the fellowship of the household of God. They are of course also characteristics of individuals who allow these gifts of the Spirit to thrive, in and through life in the community.

Wisdom has a rich and varied meaning in the biblical and theological tradition. This value is consistently seen as beginning with a relationship to God which acknowledges God's power and authority and is often spoken of as the fear (i.e. awe) of the Lord (Psalm 111). It is also recognized that the Lord gives wisdom to those who seek it. This wisdom includes the capacity to integrate understanding and action. The wise person has the skill to "bring together" the insights about how God encounters his people with concrete decisions about the reality of human life in the world. Wisdom involves faithfulness and the knowledge to apply understanding so that the gap between faith and practice is bridged in the life of the congregation and therefore in the lives of its members. Wisdom contains the root "to see"; one could say that to be wise in the Christian sense means to know where to look for the sources of God's grace when confronted with the demand to decide, act, or understand. It is the wisdom of Israel, of the church, which is the goal of our relationship to God and fellow believers. Wisdom is the aim of our interaction in Christ's name that brings integration to Christian living.

Maturity was a goal stressed by Paul in his first letter to the

Corinthians (chapters 4 and 5). It is among the mature in the faith that wisdom can be imparted. Christian adulthood, growing toward Christ, implies active participation and mutual burden bearing within the body of Christ. Full participation is accompanied by the willingness to make decisions guided by faith and to assume responsibility for the consequences of those decisions within the church and beyond its boundaries. Christian maturity is the taking on of responsibility for one's life and action within the community of faith.

Another sign of Christian maturity is the giving and receiving of support and critique within the extended family. In the congregation, Christians both force and facilitate the process of "owning" decisions of faith. Since we all have moments of immaturity and irresponsibility, we rely on the community to both sustain and restore us by speaking the truth in love.

Discernment is a special kind of perception that depends on the development of skills or capacities within the community. Discernment is the keen judgment or insight that is the basis for integrating wisdom and responsible maturity. This insight is more than knowledge, since discernment requires both intuition and sensitivity to discriminate between alternatives and their implications for faithful response. Discernment demands skills in analysis, critique, and creativity. The eye of faith seeks to analyze the crucial issues and options, to criticize constructively what has occured and the assumptions that underlie decisions, and to propose creative and compassionate alternatives for the problem encountered. Since discernment, like wisdom and maturity, is a gift of God given in community, we depend on and turn toward our brothers and sisters in Christ as we strive toward these and other goals of a vital congregation.

It should be apparent that all three goals develop a pattern of congregational life that will "increase the love of God and neighbor." Love demands that we do justice, give service, and bear the burdens not only of fellow Christians but of all persons as God's sons and daughters. The quality of relatedness in the extended family is the norm and thus consequent goal of Christian living.

2 / Using the Case Method with Families and Congregations

The Case Approach to Christian Living

> *"His divine power has granted to us all things that pertain to life and godliness. . . . For this very reason make every effort to supplement your faith with virtue, and virtue with knowledge, and knowledge with self-control, and self-control with steadfastness, and steadfastness with godliness, and godliness with brotherly affection, and brotherly affection with love." 2 Peter 1:3–7*

If our goals as a congregation are for wisdom, maturity, and discernment, the study of cases might be able to help. As indicated in this word from 2 Peter, Christian life is God's gift to the family. Our responsibility is not creating something new, but growing in the midst of God's gifts and being good stewards of his grace. These cases are presented to enable wise, mature, and discerning reflection on crucial aspects of life in the family. Bringing to bear your own experiences and ideas, your discernment and insight, upon real situations can confirm you in the valuing process and enable others to share in your efforts.

The case approach offers just one way of going about this process of growing together, but it is a good way of doing it. The case method has already been a revitalizing component in the lives of many congregations. Moreover, there is overwhelming evidence that much of the early church's decision-making was on a case-by-case basis. New Testament scholar Krister Stendhal of Harvard says that "the Bible is actually a casebook." The primary function, Stendhal suggests, of the tradition of collecting Jesus' words and stories about his acts was to address actual situations. Paul did not write general theological tracts. Rather, he applied Christ's message to specific cases within the life of the early church. The shaping of the Scriptures by "cases" is a reflection of the New Testament affirmation of the capacity of the community of faith to apply the gospel to life experience. The case method is a model of this affirmation. It is a working assumption of most case methods that there may be several responsible alternatives to human situations—differing ways to respond to the case. Response depends on a person's special insight and talents, gifts and experience. Likewise, the group studying a case together will likely be influenced by the very discussion that takes place in their process of relating to the situation. This dialogue of sharing appears to assist some communities of faith in developing a rhythm of loving and caring interaction. Interdependence within the household of God can become a normative pattern of the Christian life. We can come to rely on one another not only when there are physical needs but as sources of insight and understanding.

Some other assumptions underlie case study, and they seem likewise consonant with growth and life in Christian families:

1. The case method is student-oriented. The more participation from members of the group, the better. Participants, in their encounters with each other and their perceptions of the decision to be made, their understandings of resources and authorities, provide the basic ingredient in case study. The case teacher and the case itself help in that process. The same is true in the Christian family that believes in the "priesthood of believers" and the "communion of the saints." There is the underlying presupposition that the Holy Spirit may speak through any one of us. Case study is not only consistent with this conviction, but fosters and reinforces its application in the congregation. We learn and grow by listening to each other, thinking together, depending together on God's Spirit guiding us, and we hold that leadership only helps in that endeavor. We cannot be fully human alone. It is in the dialogue between us that Christ's Spirit is particularly present.

2. The student's religious experience and insight is ap-

preciated and respected in a case approach to learning and teaching. When life and spiritual experiences are shared, processed, and "unpacked" in dialogue, religious implications are often revealed. We fulfill Christ's command to "bear one another's burdens" by sharing ourselves. Thus it is important, both in case study in particular as in Christian living in general, not to put down another person's expression or contribution. Of course we gain by critical interaction, by being honest together. But at the heart of our enterprise is acceptance and affirmation as members of Christ's family. As Christians we seek to love our neighbor as ourselves. In so doing we affirm that we are all made in the image of God. Our brothers and sisters are accepted first for what they are, not what they do or say. The case method is intended to be "grace-full" so that God's gracious gift of life is reflected in our acceptance of those who share with us. The assumption is that the life experiences of each Christian can be a valuable mine providing benefit and profit for all the members of the Christian family.

3. The case method assumes that values and commitment are important. In the Puritan movement centuries ago, Christians used to "own the covenant" at the time they entered into full communion. They said in effect that "what I know about I now commit myself to believe in." Cases invite us to study our values and to claim those which count. Likewise in talking about what to do in a case, we do not guarantee our actions or our future behavior. But we prepare ourselves, if possible, to act and live as Christians in similar situations.

4. Case study depends on an apprenticeship/modeling pattern for learning and growth. The Christian terms are catechist and disciple, among others. We believe as Christians that we do learn orally with questions and answers, and we respond in "answers" to the questions raised by the case. More importantly, we also believe that we learn from following a "master" and seek to become ourselves truly like the teacher. In this case, we are teaching and learning from each other, seeking to apprentice ourselves to the Master—to learn from Christ-with-us in the community of faith.

Since these are rather abstract words about the case

method in Christian life, perhaps some case illustrations will help demonstrate what we mean.

Using the Case Method in Families

"We are members one of another."—Ephesians 4:25

Case study as we are doing it comes from an effort underway for six years now to explore the use of cases in theological education. Seminaries are now employing cases to study about ministry, theology, church history, ethics, and many other subjects. Case studies tend to break down the lines between traditional seminary "disciplines," and the possible gap between theological reflection and the practice of ministry. We are convinced that the case method makes for integrated, more authentic education for pastors and pastors-to-be.

Theological education is organically linked to the life of the Christian community, and now pastors are beginning to tell us of subjects that need study in seminary and suggesting cases that explore those areas of need. By the same token, many of us in seminary and church education write cases for our own and each others use when we find cases that will help.

As we seek to minister and to teach, to learn and to participate, we are finding the case method extremely helpful for a number of churches and particular groups within congregations. We offer here some illustrations from our own experience that might guide you in your efforts. Again, these are not meant to impose something from outside on your distinctive family group. Vitality seems to come from your discovering the ways in which you explore resources, these included.

A Christian Education Class for Adults. The one-hour session employed in most church school programs, whether it falls on Sunday morning or on some week night, is well-suited for the case method. Groups sometimes use cases to supplement study of a theme already under consideration. Or they will use a series of cases as material for the church school "course." One regular adult class in a suburban church, meeting on Sunday

morning, used "Carl Phillips Was Fired" as a catalyst in the
middle of their study of "Economic Concerns and the Christian
Response." Their one session with the case proved so stimulat-
ing that the class later decided to study about "Business Ethics
and the Faith," using persons and resources from their own
class identified during that case discussion.

Another congregation in the same area employed the book
by Studs Terkel, *Working,* to kick off a series on "The Biblical
Understanding of Vocation." This group of Christians examined
the effect of a job or profession on the family life of the individual and the church family. They used not only "Carl Phillips . . .," but also "The Thomas Family Goes Private," "Mary
Gardner's Fourth Pregnancy," and supplementary cases they
ordered on the topic (see p. 128 for suggestions). The eight-
week series interspersed cases with times for church members
in the group to relate their occupations to the biblical view of
work.

A natural use of this volume would be a study of "Christian
Living." The short essays on "Parish Revitalization" or "Christian Values," for example, could serve as items for discussion
and study. The essays might be assigned in conjunction with a
particular case, or they may become a starting point for your
session. The arrangement of the cases can be changed as you
seek to meet the needs and responses of your own church
group. One church group recently used eight of these cases in
a ten-week "semester." They took the first week to look at the
meaning of case study, what it offers, and how to do it. Then
they followed the case discussions with a final week of sharing
what they had learned.

Youth Group. Various churches that have tried the
method report that youth groups enjoy cases. The case method
—in fact many of the following cases—have been used with
youth conferences as well. One youth group not long ago took
four of these cases, "Westport Grass," "Thomas Family . . . ,"
"Commitment for Larry Adams," and "Youth Elder for Oak
Brook," to study together the "Roles of Youth in Church and
Family." Another tip, perhaps usable in only some youth
groups, is to allow self-leadership of the studies after a while.

Frequently, the effect of this effort has been particularly worthwhile.

One village church used a case format for youth retreats. In the fall their theme was "Values and the Family—What Shall We Stand By?" They developed "guidelines for loving" in discussions about "Dear Aunt Sarah," and "Free For—Free From." At the Spring Retreat a lively discussion of "Freedom to Grow" led the young people to organize two follow-up sessions with their parents to share in the discussion of cases on the use of drugs or alcohol and the meaning of death.

Family Retreats and Parish Programs. A case often provides an instrument for bridging differences in age and sophistication where contact with central concerns is crucial for single adults as well as for parents and children. One city congregation focused on "A Nation's Crisis of Faith" by studying the power of prayer (using a case similar to "Pray for a Miracle"), and the role of the church in changing situations, using "Mary Gardner's Fourth . . . ," to discuss abortion and "The Thomas Family . . . ," on racism and busing.

A congregation in California asked the minister to preach a series on the Ten Commandments. He, in turn, asked the congregation to study cases in special sessions. A case discussion then focused on specific commandments and he then preached on those commandments the next Sunday worship service. Cases are also an effective medium for beginning a small group or focusing discussion in a house church.

Leadership Development. A suburban congregation discovered that, for their officers' training retreat, an analysis of "Youth Elder . . ." raised the issue of officers' responsibilities as the church dealt with change, particularly as they faced a new election with a youth elder nominated for the first time. The lay governing body then voted to devote one hour of study at each monthly meeting to a different case about parish life. The case would serve as preparation for the business meeting to follow.

In that same congregation the pastor employed a number of cases with youth in a communicants' class. An evangelism task force also studied cases as did other committees.

Women's Groups and Men's Groups. We have found case

studies excellent material for circle meetings, prayer breakfasts, and for general meetings of women's and men's church groups. One young women's circle was particularly appreciative of their discussion of "Susan Carr's Decision" in which they focused on their own congregation's snub of single parents. A men's breakfast not long ago looked at "The Thomas Family." Theirs was a city where busing was being introduced that current school year.

The experiences of these groups have been good ones, by all reports. Even large groups can do case study together, as did one women's meeting recently with 150 persons in the room. Contributions were brief ones, but more than half the members actively spoke about their reactions to the case, one similar to "Pray for a Miracle."

The gift of the Holy Spirit is ultimately the only source of parish revitalization. The way in which the Spirit is a catalyst for congregational renewal varies with different types of congregations. Now that these cases are gathered and offered together, they may suggest one model for making life more abundant for those within your extended family of Christ. Application of the case method will be shaped by the history and the needs of your own congregation as well as by the time, energy, and imagination of those who seek to experiment with this educational tool. We will be eager to hear of your ideas on other ways of using cases. The address for the Case Study Institute's case production office is given in the list of resources on page 000. Most of all, we hope you will feel free to use these cases and the other resources in ways that best help your learning and Christian living. Good wishes to you in the studies.

Practical Hints for Teaching and Learning

Cases can provide surrogate experiences. Discussion of them is also meant to support growth in theological reflection and maturing faith. Nurturing patterns of support and critique will hopefully help congregations in their development of the art of loving and caring for one another—the full model of Christian living. Cases studied within the context of a supportive community are not offering "the answers" so much as "a process" for responding to situations and for facilitating personal and communal growth in wisdom, discernment, and maturity.

The role of the teacher in this process varies with the case and with the class. Ideally, the teacher is learning as much as the participants. Everyone has an opportunity to speak or listen, and the teacher simply keeps the discussion in gear. It might be the job of the teacher to set course objectives; although if that responsibility is also shared, the sessions can be "owned" more fully by all participants.

It is helpful for the teacher to have a special "game plan" for moving case discussion along. There are several approaches suggested in the study guides which follow each case. In these guides the case context has determined much about specific teaching suggestions. However, there are some basic motifs and teaching techniques discovered by experienced case teachers which you may find useful.

I. *Basic Motifs: Catalyst, Probe, and Referee*

A. Think about the leader's role in terms of a *catalyst*. Your job is to bring about a reaction in the discussion that results in more than a sheer "mixture" of participant remarks. The class discussion should break new ground, in which a "eureka!" dawns on at least a portion of those engaged in examination of the case.

Listening skills among class participants should grow, and their interaction with each other should increase. At its best, the case discussion spills over into conversations after class and personal, relational growth. Thus the image of a chemical process is a helpful one.

B. A second image is that of a *probe*. The case teacher is the asker of appropriate and illuminating questions. The study guide following each case suggests some areas for discussion, but the leader often finds that the participants introduce questions more relevant to their own situations. Participants will begin on their own to observe, analyze, reflect, and express their own theological insights. The excitement and power of cases as learning tools is in allowing and assisting students to discover for themselves not only what decision the person in the case might responsibly make but what decision the student would make in a similar situation and why. The case teacher is not seen as a dispenser of information or knowledge. Rather, he or she is a co-learner along with the students in analyzing the case and proposing responsible and creative alternatives of understanding and action.

The case method of learning and teaching is Socratic in style. It can properly be termed "interrogatory." The leader might well share insights as simple declarations, but questions are at the core of case leadership. The leader probes the collective wisdom of the class members and hopefully fosters the gaining of spiritual wisdom as well.

One caution must be added here. The case method can be unusually effective in drawing out personal reflections. The case leader must be particularly sensitive to the vulnerability of a participant who has shared some deeply personal feelings. Be gentle about applying pressure for everyone to talk. Some persons learn best listening, but others appreciate a little urging.

C. The case teacher is a *referee*. In mediating the differing perspectives and in keeping the discussion on course, the leader functions as a "game official" in some ways. As a referee you need to make certain that participants "play fair," do not attack each other or get "out of bounds" in their treatment of the subjects.

Conflict of opinion and controversy are characteristic of, and constructive in, a lively case discussion. However, some instructors have a working rule when teaching a case: "On any issue there will always be a majority of *two*—the teacher and a student under attack." Honest conflict is a great learning tool *if* the reasons for the difference of opinion are made clear. The case teacher may often wish to highlight the conflict by putting respondents in direct dialogue with one another.

One role of the teacher as referee may be periodically to remind the class to be responsible to the material at hand, even if their conclusions quite properly move beyond the situation in the case. If the instructor allows the class to speculate far beyond the data in the case or get caught up in arguing about a minor issue, this may add to the excitement but impede real progress. Some instructors find that simply to ask, "What evidence do you have that your suggestion might work?" keeps everyone honest. The student is then free to call on the case or personal experience to interpret his or her view.

Another role of the referee may be to "call time." It frequently helps to be aware of the time in dealing with cases, just as it does when one is involved in simulation games or a counseling session. An early warning of specific time limits on individual remarks will allow you the unquestioned right to interrupt the "sermonizer," the person who wants to dominate discussion with stories and moralisms.

II. *Teaching Techniques*

A. Case Preparation

Students and teacher alike have a parallel responsibility to master the case facts and comprehend the situation. Even if the case has been assigned ahead, consider taking time for everyone to reread the case before discussion begins, perhaps having a specific question in mind. You may ask the class to "Read 'Dear Aunt Sarah' once more. Try and focus this time on how Sarah Dawson must be *feeling.*"

The leader should read the printed case several times and may even make his or her outline of characters, basic issues, and a time line of events. The study guides try to list central issues. However, the leader should go beyond the guide by thinking through the various paths the case characters might take and by projecting imaginatively where the class discussion may go. The study guides are only an aid to the leader's own creative imagination.

B. Teaching the Case

Again, the study guides may suggest one possible approach to each case, but as a leader you should feel free to go beyond these suggestions. The techniques suggested for one case, such as roleplay or voting, might well be applied to others.

There are many factors which the conscientious teacher wants to keep in mind: energy levels, hostility, ignorance masked by indifference, overbearing participants, eye messages, body language, levels of insight and vocabulary, and much more. There are also a few basic techniques which experienced case leaders have found helpful in their teaching.

1. Record on the blackboard or on newsprint in a phrase or a few words what a participant contributes to the conversation. Try to use the words of a participant if possible. Check with them when you do any alteration. "Is that what you mean?" The role of interpreting and organizing participants' remarks and showing the relationship to other points is crucial for the skilled instructor. But every case teacher can hear what participants say and put their words up for all to see.

2. Try to be active in the room when appropriate. Walk to different parts of the room as discussion moves along to encourage a quiet section of the class or to focus remarks of persons upon their colleagues (not first on yourself). Remember that long silences probably belong to you to break, but brief periods of silence can also be constructive.

3. Use chair placement creatively. Arrange the chairs so people can see each other and feel free to talk back and forth. Using a "U" shape will probably be the best way to begin. But you don't have to keep chairs in one place. You can break the group into smaller ones and move the chairs into little circles. Several groups trying to work out various alternatives in the case and then attempting to persuade others is exciting but produces a sense of confusion. However, if people seem to be learning in informal conversations, you might let them proceed awhile in that manner.

4. Be conscious of your own input of experiences and insight. When you have something to say, say it. But try to keep your remarks brief. Particularly in large groups,

the leader will be standing while participants sit. You have an advantage you should not exploit. Keep in mind that this method of teaching affirms the personhood and the value of each member of the group. The leader often needs to say what he or she thinks, in sparing fashion, to preserve personal integrity. But a good leader is eager to hear what others have to contribute.

5. When you use roleplay, look for participants who give evidence in the discussion that they understand the issues and can identify with the characters in the case. Usually it helps to ask permission rather than just to assign a role to someone. This "permission" is carried through in the "deroling" process, following a roleplay where the participants' personal integrity is guarded by checking with them first: "How did you feel about the conversation? Were you comfortable with what you said?" When they have shared, the leader may turn to the other members of the group to discover what they learned from the roleplay or how they might have played the role differently.

In other instances an exciting way to heighten existential involvement with a case is to ask the entire class to assume a role, for example, of the session of the Oak Brook Church, with differing factions represented.

6. If you use the suggested technique of voting to focus the dialogue on a controversial issue, record the vote on the board. When persons are reluctant to take a position, a category of "undecided" provides a possible opportunity to test the impact of further discussion by taking another vote later on. This second vote, followed by a discussion, often brings to light the reasons which motivated people to change their votes. When this occurs the class may recognize that it is functioning as a community of interpretation, in which information and persuasion have become part of a voted, influenced exchange.

The dynamics of case teaching reveal that a decision point may be clarified by pushing persons to decide and to defend their views. Many instructors also use the vote to probe for implicit reasons and assumptions that stand behind a given decision.

C. Concluding the Case

Especially as a session nears its conclusion, the leader might encourage the class to build on the suggestions of one another, sketch concrete alternative solutions, and then critically compare these alternatives and their consequences. It is often easier for a group to keep the discussion primarily in the area of analysis of case characters or their situations. Particularly if the group is new to the case approach, the leader may need to urge the class to work beyond the persons to the *implications* of the possible solutions being suggested.

In concluding a case or providing a wrap-up, some case leaders also find it constructive to ask the participants what they have learned from one another and then list these learnings as a communal summary. However, on other occasions the leader may appropriately have important insights or an integrative way of understanding the case or issue that he or she has a responsibility to share. The pattern of identifying these contributions as the concerns of the instructor and thus distinguishing them from any suggestion that this is *the* solution is, most case teachers find, an important element in the learning experience. Some leaders introduce their own summary style which says, "This way of thinking about the case interests me and so I share it with you. Try it on and see if it fits the case. If not, discard it." Remember that part of the excitement and power of cases lies in the ability of participants to discover for themselves not only what decisions the persons in the case might make, but what decisions *they* would make and why.

PART II
Cases, with Study Guides

3 / The Family: Guidelines for Loving

Freedom to Grow

As Mary Johnson sat by the telephone, she could hear her 15-year-old daughter Katie crying in the next room. The night before, Katie's date, Mike Fedson, had been picked up on suspicion of drunken driving as he was bringing Katie home from a local high school club party. Mike was 18. He was taken to police headquarters and the couple with whom Katie was double dating had brought her home at 3:00 A.M.

When Katie had come down to breakfast that morning, she told her mother she was sorry about worrying her so much the night before. Katie said that if she had called from the police station she was afraid her parents would have been even more concerned. Mary was still quite upset and told Katie she was going to call the party chaperones. Mary reminded Katie that when she had agreed to let a 15-year-old go to this particular party with a much older boy, she had been assured that no alcohol was allowed at the party. Mary told Katie that she was also considering calling a meeting of a number of the parents of the young people in Katie's crowd.

At this point, Katie had broken down in tears. "Why do you want to embarrass me so much? It's not any of your business what the other kids do. That's up to *their* parents. I don't drink. I think its stupid. But everybody else drinks and what I say about it wouldn't make any difference.

"Look, Mother. Mike had only a few beers in the parking lot. He wasn't drunk. On our way home the police stopped him to check on his driver's license and they smelled alcohol on his breath. That's all. It's not so serious. We weren't in an accident or anything like that. You're blowing this whole thing up too big. If you call all my friends' parents and make a big thing out of all this, I won't have any friends left at all, and for sure I won't have another date for the rest of my life!" Katie had run into her room crying and slammed the door.

Mary Johnson was still determined to call one of the adult chaperones for the club party and learn why drinking had been allowed. Ted Mallory responded with cold, crisp logic. "My wife and I were asked to be present at the party, admit no alcoholic beverages, and generally supervise the kids there in the clubhouse. What goes on out in the parking lot during that party is none of our business. This goes on at all the parties. You've got to give the kids some room to grow up. It's crazy to think about supervising them every minute. The seniors will be in jobs or in college in a few more months. It's better to let them learn to handle the alcohol now than when they're completely on their own. We're forty-five miles from the state line. If we don't let the teenagers drink here, they'll drive into the next state where the legal age is only eighteen, three years younger than here, and get killed driving home. Come on, Mary, I know you and Bruce both drink socially. Why should it be different for the kids?" Ted Mallory hung up the phone with a definite "click."

Mary later said she really had wanted to tell Mallory off. "Sure, he was logical," Mary reasoned, "but the blunt truth of the matter is that letting those kids buy liquor is as illegal and irresponsible as Mike's driving when he had been drinking. I'm not trying to raise Katie in a cocoon, but kids need some clear limits until they are mature enough to make responsible decisions. Allowing them to break the law and slip around the rules isn't the way to go about it."

After the call to Ted Mallory, Mary sat back and tried to sort out what she saw as the options before her. She remembered that Katie's father had been equally disturbed this morning before he left for the office. He was quite angry with Mike Fedson and suggested that Katie should never be allowed to go out with him again. Bruce said to Mary at the time, "Maybe our decision to let Katie date a boy that much older or go to these club parties was a mistake after all. I don't know if Katie asked him not to drink or even if that would have made any difference. I want Katie to know that we trust her, but it's not fair to let her get into situations she can't handle at her age."

Mary was hesitant to tell Katie she could neither go to the parties nor date Mike anymore. Katie had been dating him for several weeks, he was from a nice family, and had always seemed courteous. Katie was just beginning to gain some confidence in herself, and to be perfectly frank, she seemed to be thriving on the special "prestige" of dating an older boy. Mary thought, "If Bruce and I tell Katie she can no longer see Mike, that could put a real barrier between us. Forcing Katie to see Mike in secret might turn into an exciting game that would be terribly destructive to her relationship with us. We've tried to give Katie more freedom than our parents ever gave us. But maybe Bruce is right. The old-fashioned limits might be the best thing for Katie.

"I guess what is *really* underneath the issue of Katie's dating is my wider concern for the whole crowd of teenagers who not only see drinking as a smart thing to do but can attend organized parties where they are allowed to drink freely, even if that's outside and not inside. I don't want to be the kind of mother who constantly interferes with her child's life, but I do want to do the most loving and responsible thing for Katie as well as the other youngsters involved. Maybe what our minister said at church on Sunday about the difference between real freedom and license and what it means to really love someone is at stake here. Wouldn't a meeting of some of the parents to talk over the issues be better than restricting Katie? Or would she be so hurt by my taking a step like this, that it would do more harm to Katie than good? What if I find out that it doesn't make any difference to the other parents after all?"

The hard logic of Ted Mallory and the sound of Katie sobbing in the next room made Mary hesitate before she started to look up the first number.

Freedom to Grow
Study Guide

The life of the family is the location in which a decision must be made in the three cases of this section. In each of these the immediate or nuclear family provides the primary context in which value formation occurs. Modeling within the family— for better or for worse—has already affected the members of these families. Other areas for modeling, such as the church, culture, and the wider concerns of humanity, also influence the cases, but these areas will become the focus of interest in later sections.

The biblical and theological tradition as interpreted by the church has highlighted a number of values or qualities which have been judged worthy of shaping the pattern of Christian living. Faith, hope, and love are the principal values, but other characteristics of life flow from these sources. Love has been frequently understood as the determining Christian value. The two greatest commandments according to Jesus were to "love the Lord your God with all your heart, and with all your soul, and with all your strength" and to "love your neighbor as yourself." A modern theologian has suggested the purpose of the church is "to increase the love of God and neighbor." However, love in different situations demands different responses. One approach to the discussion of the first three cases would be to explore the idea of value formation for families through the development of Guidelines for Loving.

This first discussion guide and teaching note will suggest this as one option, although other themes such as freedom or responsibility could equally command the attention of a dialogue and will naturally be sub-themes within this teaching note as well.

I. *Implications of the Decision*

After opening the discussion with a prayer of gratitude for the family, the community, and the freedom to make a responsible decision in light of the problem facing the Johnson family, the discussion leader may wish to clarify the basic information in the case. This could be done by exploring the *implications* of the decision Mary must make: whether or not to phone the other parents.

A. How might her decision affect Katie, Katie's relationship with Mike, with her peers, and the relationship of Katie to her parents?

B. How will the quality of communication between Katie and her parents in this situation or a future crisis be influenced by Mary's decision and why?

C. What do you think troubles Bruce or Mary most about what Katie and Mike did? The hour? Drinking and driving? The encounter with the police? Disobedience?

D. Should Mary make a decision by herself, or only after consultation with Bruce, other parents including Ted Mallory, Katie, Mike and the other young people, or other resource persons? This style of discussion should allow the facts and feelings concerning the case to surface.

II. *Basic Values Reflected*

Issues raised in this case provide the opportunity to explore and clarify the meaning of ones basic commitments. These include:

A. **Freedom.** What are the levels and the limits of freedom appropriate for Katie and/or Mike? Is it responsible for the Johnsons to limit Katie's freedom? If so, should that involve negotiation with her or only clear expectations? Where would you place Katie on a continuum or line between these opposites: total control————license? One might ask persons to give their judgment and explain why they chose that location. How does this relate to the high value Paul placed on freedom given us in Christ and the responsibility that freedom places on us for the care of others (Gal. 5:13–15)?

B. **Responsibility.** What are the various responsibilities of each of the five characters? List and compare them. Do the boundaries of these responsibilities change with circumstances and age? Is there a responsibility to facilitate another's sense of freedom and capacity to love?

C. Trust. How can Bruce and Mary let Katie know they trust her? Specifically, how would their faith in Katie get communicated to her if faith means a relationship of trust and loyalty? Does loving trust involve protection or allowing one you love to make his/her own mistakes? Consider having two persons roleplay Katie and her father discussing these ideas for a few minutes. Then ask the group as a whole to respond (see "Practical Hints on Teaching," p. 37).

III. *Alternatives Available*

Case discussion should stimulate a number of creative options for responding to this family crisis. Options are always informed by what one values, and the alternative should incorporate or strengthen that commitment to values. Ask members of the group to share how they would solve this dilemma and to give briefly the reasons for their recommendation. The instructor might list the options and rationale, urging the group to be specific.

A. Some options which have arisen in the authors' discussions of "Freedom to Grow" are:

1. Mary should postpone the call until after a family conference involving Katie/Mary/Bruce/sometimes Mike. The contact with other parents and peers remains an option emerging from this conference.
2. Consult with the pastor or other counselor.
3. Call for an open meeting of all the parents.

B. In any of these options some basic guidelines for a *loving response* may involve the following themes:

1. Trust and love are communicated in the style of conversations which respect the importance and age of each person present, and shared responsibility for the negotiated solution rests with all as feelings, failures, and hopes are exchanged by parents and children.
2. The issues of hours, drinking, and dating age, and honesty and proper obligations to other members of the family are discussed and tested as family values that involve accountability *and* forgiveness when not met.

3. Modeling for and by the community might be explored as a means of mutual clarification of and support for certain types of behavior by youth and adults that affirm growth toward maturity, freedom, and increasing responsibilities. An open community meeting of concerned parents might foster this approach.

IV. *Locations of Grace*

Whatever decisions are made by members of the Johnson family, the discussion of their case hopefully will identify some resources for addressing life cases with similar issues. These resources might be called by Christians "locations of grace." This refers to God's grace that supplies the gifts of persons, concepts, and sources of faith that may assist one in making responsible and loving decisions. Ask the group what they suggest would aid the Johnsons in their response to this situation. Other groups have noted factors which include:

A. Relationships between members of the family—mutual resources to one another.

B. Christian faith and doctrine which see trust in God as the basis for trust in his other children. Freedom in Christ which is the foundation for liberation with care for others and a new form of maturity.

C. The church as the extended family of God may provide support and critique for the whole family and special counsel if desired.

D. The community itself in terms of other concerned parents and youth, school counselors and officials, and law enforcement officers and drug interpretation personnel.

E. Prayer which seeks the presence and guidance of the Holy Spirit for the personal relationships and wisdom in deciding.

V. *Initial Guidelines for Loving*

The concrete demands of love vary in each instance but some persistent factors seem to remain. One may ask the discussion group to summarize their learnings from the case by listing their own guidelines for loving and the relation if any to the values affirmed and formed in the Christian tradition. Other groups have suggested guidelines which include the following, which you may want to compare to your group's list:

    Trust as a foundation
    Mutual respect
    Mutual responsibility
    Promotion of freedom
    Compassionate acknowledgement of needs, promises,
    & failures

VI. *Use of the Case*

This discussion guide and teaching note has been particularly but not exclusively designed for considering "Freedom to Grow" as the first case in a study of Christian Living. In that instance you might want to precede the discussion session on this case with a consideration of one of the introductory essays. The articles on "What Is Christian Living?" or "Christian Values" might provide an interesting ground breaking approach. The Introduction will provide some preliminary information on the case method. "Freedom to Grow" has been used successfully with adults and young people; it is particularly helpful in encouraging cross-generational dialogue. It has been especially useful when employed in a retreat or family camp setting. The essay on "Modeling as a Process" is a good bridge to other cases such as "Dear Aunt Sarah" or "Free From—Free For," which both illustrate the impact of value shaping within the family.

VII. *Suggested Additional Reading*

Erich Fromm, *The Art of Loving* (New York: Harper & Row), 1974, paperback; and C.S. Lewis, *Four Loves* (New York: Harcourt Brace Jovanovich), 1971, paperback.

Dear Aunt Sarah

Connie Arnold looked at her husband Jim as she handed him the third letter in two weeks from Aunt Sarah. They both knew they had to respond in the next couple of days to Sarah Dawson's request to come and live with their family.

Connie and Jim sat down in the living room with the three letters and tried to think through the situation. Aunt Sarah was Connie's mother's older sister. Her husband George had died four years ago. George and Sarah Dawson had no children. Now that Connie's parents were both dead, the Arnolds were Sarah's only living relatives. Two years after George died, Sarah had sold their house and had rented a little apartment in the same neighborhood. Jim and Connie knew that Aunt Sarah had a small but livable income from George's pension plan and that interest from investment of the sale of the house just covered her rent.

Connie read aloud two paragraphs from Aunt Sarah's first letter:

> It is always my greatest joy to see you, Jim, and those three beautiful children of yours. I know what a long drive it is out here to Appleton—almost three hours. Though I remember when I was a girl the trip took over seven hours on the train. I know how busy you are, but with George and all of our friends gone now, the weeks seem so long between your visits.
>
> Even though I am 78, I'm still a spry old girl. Connie, I know you have talked about getting a job. I do not approve of a mother being out of her home, but if you're set on it, I would be glad to come and live with you to take care of little Joel when he comes home from school. A seven-year-old still needs a lot of loving.

Connie later told Jim she was a bit surprised by Aunt Sarah's offer. She had thought that "absolutely nothing" would pull Sarah Dawson away from Appleton. Rather, Connie assumed this was really Aunt Sarah's way of showing her unhappiness over the job issue. Connie had responded to the letter by writing that she hadn't yet decided on going back to work and that if she did, it would only be part time and that Anne, their 14-year-old, would also be at home when Joel got out of school.

Aunt Sarah's second letter came by return mail:

> I've been thinking about all the work you and Jim have done on your house. I remember you had wanted to fix up that top floor for a long time. The two bedrooms for Anne and Susan sound very nice and I know how glad they are to finally have their own separate den and a bathroom. With Susan going away to college this year, you'll have a lot of extra room. It doesn't make much sense to me to pay rent for this apartment when I could be giving you and Jim all that money for Susan's empty room. Anne will be lonely up there by herself.

Before Connie could answer this letter, a third one from Aunt Sarah arrived in the mail two days later.

> I've been thinking that it might be hard for us all to manage in your little kitchen. I still have most of the money from the sale of our house. I'll be glad to pay to convert a section of the new den into a nice little kitchen for Anne and myself.
>
> Though I have been so well, I think I had another little heart spell last night. You remember my George died of a heart attack. I told Fluffy and Meow that we will be moving soon, so they need not be afraid of anything happening to me all alone.

After rereading the last line, Jim burst out, "Connie, as dearly as I love Aunt Sarah, I don't see how we could survive with those two obnoxious cats of hers. Our old beagle Sam would turn this house into a combat zone."

"Now, Jim," Connie responded quickly, "you and I both know we don't want to make a decision like this based on two cats. We're the only ones Aunt Sarah has left. I think of all the beautiful summers I spent as a child with Uncle George and Aunt Sarah. And it was Uncle George who really supported my last two years of college. Now I feel it's my turn to be on the giving end."

Jim answered slowly, "Connie, I don't know how we can ask Susan to give up her room after she has waited seven years to have a place of her own. And even if she agrees, I don't want her to feel that because she's going away to college, she no longer has a place in our home. And do you really believe that an active 14-year-old is going to thrive with Sarah pouring vitamins down her throat, telling her to turn down—or off—the stereo, and wanting to go to bed at 8 o'clock? We've expanded this house as much as possible, and on my salary a bigger one is out of the question.

"I know the kids love Sarah, but they run to the car when it's time to come back home after visits. You told me yourself that on our last trip home Susan whispered to you that she thought Aunt Sarah was 'really neat' but her 'remembering the old days' was enough to drive Susan 'up the wall.'

"Connie, I'm not trying to be so negative. I do agree that we have some responsibility for Sarah and she has a folksy wisdom that I respect. I just want us to be clear about the pressures Sarah would introduce. In a few years she may not be able to get around at all. This would dramatically change our lives if she is living here with us."

Connie nodded her head. "Jim, I'm not naïve about the problems. Aunt Sarah lives in another era. It is particularly hard for me to deal with her strong and constant disapproval of my decision to get a job, and I'm sure that would carry over into other areas of our lifestyle. But what other options are there? I don't see how she could afford any decent apartment here in the city without cutting into the principal of her savings. You and I both know that's her only emergency resource beyond Medicare. There is no way we could afford a nursing home and I don't think she would even consider that. On our last visit she told me with real anger about old Mrs. Robbins who moved into the home in Appleton. Aunt Sarah said Eulie Robbins' children had 'committed her to the grave.'

"Jim, I've already mentioned the idea of Aunt Sarah living here to each of the children, but I'm not clear what we're really asking them. I feel a deep love and responsibility for Sarah. I think we all do. But I also feel it's a decision the whole family has to make and not just the two of us."

Connie Arnold looked down at the almost blank sheet of stationery in her hands. So far the only words were "Dear Aunt Sarah, . . ."

Dear Aunt Sarah
Study Guide

This case could focus on how Guidelines for Loving apply to situations within the extended family. Some of the primary issues you may want to focus on are those of Christian *responsibility:* what are our obligations to those in the extended family?; and Christian *freedom:* what limits do the needs of others place on us and how is the Christian *free* to respond to those in need?

I. *Facts and Feelings of a Decision*

A. One way to enter discussion would be to ask the class to consider what role or "stake" each of the persons has in making the decision about Aunt Sarah. What are the facts and feelings for each person? For example, Connie: Is Sarah's niece, loves her, feels obligated, is worried about intrusion. Aunt Sarah: Would leave her hometown, might contribute funds, is lonely, worried. Discuss and list for each.

Whose responsibility is it to make the decision? Is there any one person more responsible than another?

B. At this point you might ask the participants to put themselves in the place of one of the members of the family and vote on whether or not Sarah Dawson should move in. (See Practical Hints, p. 000). Record the vote with a space for "undecided," then ask class members to explain why they voted as they did. This could lead to a discussion of *criteria* for decision making.

II. *Criteria*

For any of those persons involved, what are some of the basic *criteria* for making the decision about Sarah Dawson?

Listed below are some of the possible responses the class may give.

  A. The financial situation

    1. Sarah: Has a modest and limited income, would contribute rent money and second kitchen.

    2. Arnolds: Middle income family, limited resources, concerned about Sarah as future medical burden.

    3. How important *should* the economics be? Is this a primary factor in loving and caring? Why or why not?

  B. Freedom

    1. If she moved, would *Sarah* be freer? (from worry or loneliness?) Would she give up any freedoms in adjusting to life with a young family?

    2. Connie: Would Sarah's coming free her to go back to work? Would Connie feel guilty about going to work, knowing Sarah's feelings about it?

    3. The children: How might their freedom be limited by Sarah? Could Sarah "expand" their horizons and somehow free them to be open to new ways of relating to others?

    4. Does freedom mean doing whatever you want to do when you want to? Can you be "free" and "responsible" at the same time?

    This question might lead to a discussion of the criteria of the following.

  C. Responsibility

If Sarah comes, what are the *responsibilities* involved for the characters?

    1. Consider what responsibilities Sarah has offered to assume. Why do you think Sarah has approached the Arnolds this way? Is it because one no longer feels *worthwhile* unless he/she is giving? Is this good? The group might consider here the Christian theme of affirming one's personhood because of who they *are* and not by what they *do*.

    2. How do Connie and Jim Arnold see their responsibilities as Sarah's only relative? What adjustments to their present lifestyle would be demanded? What responsibili-

ties do they have if Sarah does or does not move in?
3. Do you see any areas of responsibility for the children?
Change in lifestyle if Sarah comes? What does this mean?
What burdens, if any, should they assume?

III. *Response*

A. Guidelines for loving. In light of the categories of eco-
nomics, freedom, and responsibility, what do you consider the
most *loving* response to Sarah Dawson? Consider that being
loving may mean being *open* to many different alternatives as
well as being open to the Holy Spirit.

B. Alternatives. Some available options are: (1) a "trial visit"
from Sarah; (2) a small apartment near the Arnolds; (3) saying
"no" to Sarah at this time; (4) accepting Sarah's request either
with or without "conditions"; (5) explore nursing home option.
One helpful technique to clarify mutual learnings here may be
to call for a second vote from the group on the decision about
Aunt Sarah. Has anyone changed his/her mind? Why or why
not?

C. Communication. Think about how Sarah and the Arnolds might *feel* with each of these options. Consider the fact
that the way the Arnolds communicate with Sarah may be as
important as their final decision. Should they consult or tell
Sarah? Should they write, phone her, go for a visit? What do you
think is the most important thing for the Arnolds to communicate? Why?

IV. *Resources of Grace*

What kind of help does the Christian faith offer the Arnolds?

A. Biblical. Discuss the biblical notion of the extended family as a cherished obligation (e.g. Acts 2:43–47, 4:32–37). Also
Paul (Rom. 12:9–13) calls on Christians who care for others to
do so with "genuine love," "zeal," and "cheerfulness." How can
Christian responsibility become a joy and not a burden? Paul
also talks about being called to freedom (Gal. 5:13) in which the
law is fulfilled by loving your neighbor "as yourself." What does
this freedom mean to a Christian?

B. Support Community. Is the Arnold family or the church a possible location of grace? Are there others in the Appleton or city community to whom Sarah and the Arnolds can turn? How could a community of peers help Sarah? Has a community in dialogue helped any members in your group reach a decision about Aunt Sarah?

C. Prayer and Pastoral Care. Individual prayer or prayers of the community provide a resource. What would be a loving and responsible prayer for Sarah, the Arnolds, or the members of their church?

V. *Use of the Case*

The discussion of "Dear Aunt Sarah" could be accompanied by a consideration, perhaps in small groups, of the essay on "Christian Living in the Early Church." Can the model of the Holy Spirit's presence and the expression of the Christian's concern and care for one another be applied to a modern congregation? How might that be done? A family retreat, officers' planning session (particularly with deacons or those charged with the pastoral care of others), or gatherings of a parish group might provide an opportunity to employ the case apart from regular Christian Education.

VI. *Suggested Additional Reading*

Donald F. Clingan, *Aging Persons in the Community of Faith* (Indiana Commission on the Aging and Aged), 1975. Order this paperback from the Christian Board of Publications, Box 179, St. Louis, Missouri 63116. Philip Slater, *The Pursuit of Loneliness: American Culture at the Breaking Point* (Boston: Beacon Press), 1976, paperback.

Free For—Free From

Fran Reynolds turned away from her husband Jim and looked toward the group of friends surrounding them. "Over the past six years you've all come to know Jim and me pretty well. You've seen us both share, but for months now you've seen us fight bitterly and grow further apart. You were all a part of what happened here tonight. I never knew I could feel close enough to any group of people to trust them with such a painful issue. But I think we really need your help. Should Jim and I seriously think about divorce?"

James Reynolds turned and walked out of the room. The front door slammed, and moments later the sound of a roaring motor and screeching tires cut through the evening. Tom Holland, a friend of many years, stood and said he needed to go find Jim. He squeezed Fran's hand as he hurried out of the room.

In the quiet that followed Fran's question and the departure of the two men, Sharon Holland, Tom's wife and also a close friend of the Reynolds, mentally retraced the background and events of the evening.

The group of five couples, with a few changes due to two couples moving away and two others invited to participate, was now in its seventh year of bimonthly meetings. Though not officially a church-sponsored group, they all were members of the same Protestant congregation. The group consisted of two businessmen, a physician, a lawyer, the church's pastor, and their wives, three of whom had careers in the fields of teaching or counseling. The couples had spent evenings on personal concerns and contemporary articles as well as in discussion of prayer and Bible study. The leadership for discussion rotated throughout the group. Tonight the meeting had been scheduled at Tom and Sharon Holland's home; the primary topic for the evening was "freedom."

Almost an hour after the group had finished coffee and begun sharing their ideas and feelings, Jim Reynolds arrived. Though not drunk, he appeared "well-oiled," as Sharon had whispered to Tom. Jim had been away on business for five days and had come straight from the airport as he and Fran had planned. Fran had been talking to the group about the master's course in guidance and counseling she was pursuing at a local college. Her interest in the field had been sparked initially by a couples' retreat three years earlier which involved transactional analysis.

Though Jim had participated in that first retreat and had shared with the other participants some deep feelings of rejection by his own father, he had said at the time that the analytical process was "fruitless" for him. In subsequent group encounters Jim was often willing to discuss negative aspects of his childhood or problems with his children, but he usually concluded by stating that he was a "man of action" who found his "real gratification in his work, in success," and not in "all this digging around in the past." Sharon Holland had agreed with Jim's analysis. He was indeed a "man of action." Not long after the Reynolds moved to the Fairfield, Michigan community, Jim had been instrumental in founding the Fairfield Junior Chamber of Commerce. He had also participated actively in a Boy Scout program with his son Sam. Both Jim and Fran were quite involved in the church, Jim having just completed a three-year term as a church officer this past January. Four years ago he and Fran were integral to the success of a flourishing community/ church teen group. Jim had even written poetry for a while; Sharon felt that it, too, was active, issue-oriented . . . never introspective.

Sharon's thoughts turned to Fran Reynolds, who had become increasingly involved, as she termed it, in "the creative potential of self-analysis," primarily through transactional analysis. Other members of the couples group had confirmed that Fran worked at "getting in touch with herself" and improving her relationships to others. Fran had also shared a number of times how important her prayer life and her acceptance by this group of friends were in her attempts to change.

Earlier in the evening when Fran was speaking enthusiastically about the new courses, Sharon reflected on the tremendous change the past three years had brought to Fran's whole outlook on life. Rather than the stance of "depressed submission" that Sharon felt had once characterized Fran, Sharon now saw her "eager to understand herself and deal with life." As the group had previously discussed, Fran's change in attitude was clearly reflected in her attempts to work creatively with the problems of at least one of their two children.

Beth, the eldest child, had been born ten months after Fran and Jim were married. Two years ago, Fran had shared with the group how much she had resented the baby. "Every time she cried, I just stuffed her with food." Beth, now fourteen years old at 140 pounds and quite fat for her 5'3" height, was a quiet child, an avid reader who had few friends. However, during the past two years Fran had begun to work seriously on her relationship with Beth. They now often shopped together, they had worked to redecorate Beth's room, and Fran had encouraged Beth to take tennis lessons with her.

Sam was born eleven months after Beth. Both Fran and Jim had brought some of his problems to the group. Now in the seventh grade, Sam was in constant trouble and was feared as a "bully" by the smaller neighborhood children. Though tests had shown him to be a very bright boy, Sam's marks were barely passing. There had been several instances in the past four years when Jim had stayed home from work to deal with Sam's truancy and other misbehavior at school.

The children became part of the conversation after Jim entered into the evening discussion. Responding to the theme of "freedom" and Fran's discussion of her courses, Jim had said, "I feel that I have certainly allowed you to be free to develop yourself." Fran had answered immediately, "You haven't *given* me anything that wasn't mine in the first place."

Jim's voice had grown louder. "In the *first* place you chose to have a family and that should be your first priority. At least one of our children is in real trouble and I seem to be the person who has to come home and straighten things out. I give my soul to that office to make enough money to *let* you spend your time at home with those children. Your pursuing a career at this time is selfish and may even be destructive to children who depend on you."

Fran had taken a deep breath and responded slowly. "Just why you think those children are my responsibility alone is a mystery to me. We've *both* been a part of messing them up and, with God's grace, we should both be a part of helping them to straighten out. I don't know if you come home to help Sam or to make me feel guilty. Jim, I don't want to raise those children alone. I need you for them and I need you for me. But we need a real piece of you and not just your angry presence popping in and out.

"You're exactly right when you say you give your soul to that office. Maybe five years ago our clothes, the house, and those fancy sports cars of yours were important to me and I saw your work as a necessary means to those objects. But they're not important to me anymore. Now I see them as objects that put us in debt and keep us there. Your obsession with business and material success is all yours. You've been competing with your father since the day you were born. Don't hang that one on me!"

Jim's voice had shaken as he first whispered and then responded more loudly. "That's what's really at the bottom of all this. For months I've talked about wanting to move to the Chicago suburbs to live on my father's property and you've fought me all the way. He's an old man. I'll be damned if I'm going to let him cut me off and give my three insipid, doting sisters two thousand acres of prime land that's rightfully mine."

"Jim, I'll move tomorrow if you can face a terrible need within yourself to heal some deep, life-long wounds in your relationship with your father. But that crass, blind rationalization about land and money is no reason to rip a family away from friends and a home of ten years."

Jim stood and looked down at Fran, his voice choked with emotion. *"You're* calling *me* blind! Three years ago when I was transferred to the main office in Chicago, I was willing to let the family stay here in Fairfield so I now commute over an hour to work. That's not because I enjoy spending three hours of every day behind the wheel. You've never had any appreciation for my decision."

"It's impossible to say 'thank you' when you ram it down my throat three hours of every day," Fran retorted.

Jim grabbed the back of the chair and shouted, "Why is it

that somehow *I'm* always the bad guy? Fran, you've always been a weak, dependent little girl. I try and make you stand on your own two feet, face some of the cold, hard realities of your responsibilities as a wife and mother, and you turn around and become dependent on indulgent people who call themselves friends. You've really got them all fooled, haven't you? Poor little Fran. They're the ones you need now. Not me."

"Maybe that's right, Jim. I may need them now more than I need you. I swear it's not the way I want it. I am trying to change and grow, but you won't let me. We may now be so destructive of one another and of our children that continuing to live together is wrong for us as well as the children."

It was then, with tears in her eyes, that Fran turned to the hushed group around them. . . . Sharon Holland felt that Fran was speaking directly to her.

Free For—Free From
Study Guide

If the nuclear family is a focus for modeling and value formation, what happens in a situation of conflict? Divorce is perhaps the most dramatic example of conflict in the family. The increasing rate of divorce in the U.S., and the effect it has on those involved, indicates the importance of exploring guidelines for loving in situations of conflict. Churches have taken different official and unofficial stands on divorce. Almost every church has understood the division of the family to be serious and tragic given the biblical and theological support for marriage (1 Cor. 7:10–11). Yet almost every church recognizes certain conditions under which divorce appears to be the least destructive action. Perhaps most significantly, many communities of faith have acknowledged the reality of divorce and asked how they can respond to a divided family with support and critique. One of the most frequent reasons given for divorce seems to be the "need to be free." Perhaps this case will allow a group to explore together the meaning of such issues as love in conflict, the need for freedom from and freedom for another person, and creative ways to resolve the two. Rather than siding on the "right" or "wrong" of a particular decision, you may be able to focus on the most loving response Christians can give to those in conflict.

I. *Free For—From Sharing*

The discussion might begin by asking if Fran Reynolds was fair to Jim in raising the issue of divorce with a group of friends. Do you think Jim and Fran had discussed this before? What was the emotional situation when Fran turned to the group? There are private areas of a relationship between two people. Should there be any limits on sharing? Why or why not? What does it mean to speak of love as "mutual trust"? How do your answers apply to the conflict between Fran and Jim Reynolds?

II. *Free For—From the Past*

Each of our lives has been shaped by experiences and by models in our past. Christians affirm that Christ frees us from sins of the past, binding elements which prevent a more open and loving relationship to God and to others. We may become free for a more abundant life, a new way of relating to others. This does not mean, however, that the past "never happened" or is not crucial to who we are. One of the central issues for Jim and Fran may be both to accept and to break free from the past.

A. What would being free from the past mean to Fran? How is she trying to achieve this? Jim is a "man of action." Is he affected by his past? How does he deal with his past?

What does Fran mean when she says that "we both messed up" the children? How could Jim or Fran help their children look on their problems in a new way?

B. Being free *for* the past may involve accepting that persons are products of their pasts, which may include hidden potential. Loving often means accepting a person unconditionally, even if that person changes. How might this criteria affect the relationship between Jim and Fran? Has she accepted his past? Has he accepted her new attitudes and attempts to break away from old patterns? Why or why not?

III. *Free For—From Others*

There is often a tension between responsibility to ourselves and to others. For many women in our culture this tension is evident in the conflict between the development of a woman's own potential and the fulfillment of previously accepted responsibilities to others, especially children. How would you help Fran Reynolds evaluate her priorities? To what extent may Fran need to be free from the children? How can she be free *for* them? Apply these same questions to Jim. Do Fran and Jim understand their responsibilities to each other? Why or why not?

Does the couples group have any responsibility for Fran and Jim? Consider the obligations of respect, support, critique. Is the group ultimately responsible for what happens to Jim and Fran? Why or why not? Paul reminds us that through Christ "we have been allowed to enter the sphere of God's grace, where we now stand." (Rom. 5:2, N.E.B.) How might an understanding of God's grace be helpful here?

IV. *Free For—From the Future*

In what ways could the group offer assistance to Fran and Jim? (Have they already?) Consider a roleplay between Fran and Sharon Holland, taking up the situation at the end of the case. This could be followed by a roleplay between Jim Reynolds and Tom Holland.

What support would the Reynolds need if they divorce? If they continue to live together?

V. *Resources for Freedom in Grace*

What are the resources to which both Fran and Jim may look for help? What are the possibilities and limitations here? The group may consider:

A. Jim and Fran look to each other. Current conflict makes them against and not for one another, thus limiting both. Are there ways to resolve the immediate tension?

B. The couples group. Is Fran dependent on the group or freed by it? Why does Jim see the group as a threat? Are there ways to resolve this?

C. The pastor. Is his experience in counseling a possible resource? What effect might his being in the group have on the situation?

D. Prayer and the need for forgiveness. What role could forgiveness play in this case?

VI. *Use of the Case*

This case can be used effectively in koinonia groups and family retreats as well as for marriage enrichment seminars. The essays on "Parish Revitalization" and "Goals for Congregational Life" may provide helpful preparation.

VII. *Suggested Additional Reading*

Elizabeth Achtemeier, *The Committed Marriage* (Philadelphia: Westminster Press), 1976, paperback; Rollo May, *Love and Will* (New York: Dell), 1974, paperback; and Granger Westberg, *Good Grief* (Philadelphia: Fortress Press), 1976, paperback.

4 / The Church: Guidelines for Trusting

Carl Phillips Was Fired

Carl Phillips walked back to his car after leaving Mary Matthews' house. His mind was reeling with the jarring awareness that he might have been able to prevent the death of Mary's husband and his friend, Tom Matthews.

Carl had known Mary and Tom almost 10 years, both through Tom's organizational work on the Scarsdale little league baseball team and through the church. Carl was an active deacon in their congregation and had called on the Matthews in the past on regular church business. As soon as he learned of Tom's suicide, Carl had gone immediately to the Matthews home.

As Carl drove slowly home he recalled his conversation with Mary. Carl thought he had known Tom Matthews pretty well but was now aware that he actually knew very little about him. Mary had confided that in the past few months Tom had had an increasing problem with alcohol, that he was frequently depressed, and was basically unable to accept being "phased out" of his executive position in a large New York firm six weeks ago. Carl repeated to himself what he had told Mary, "If I'd only known. . . ."

Carl Phillips was also being "phased out" of his managerial position in a New York advertising concern quite similar to Tom Matthews'. Carl thought back about his own reactions six months ago when he was first notified that in the next three months his department of fifteen men would be drastically cut back to nine. At first Carl had fought for his job, appealing to personal friends higher up on the executive "ladder." He had an impressive record as an innovative designer. Carl received a further three-month extension, but now knew that the total company financial picture was all too clear. He would be one of the six men to go. His last salary check would come in two weeks.

Those first few months he had written literally hundreds of job applications, sent resumes, followed newspaper job advertisements, been to employment agencies, and was becoming increasingly depressed by the employment situation. There were simply no jobs around in advertising or otherwise for a man over forty.

Carl had not told his wife Marilyn that he was losing his job until three weeks ago. Their two teenage sons were pretty independent now and for the first time in fifteen years Marilyn had gone back to work. Not a very impressive salary, but Carl felt the job was giving her a new sense of confidence.

Carl wondered again why he had waited to long to tell her. "Marilyn is a pretty emotional person," he thought. "I guess I was afraid how she would take it. As a matter of fact, that was a pleasant surprise. She's coping much better than I had expected.

"I guess it was also my male ego. I've been conditioned from childhood that the father is the head of the household and the provider of the family."

It was on Marilyn's insistence that neither she nor Carl had told their boys about the job loss. Marilyn had stressed that there was no need to burden the children with their parents' problems. The boys had enough to deal with in school.

When Carl reached home he found Marilyn in the kitchen. It was Saturday and the boys were on an overnight hike. Carl told Marilyn what he had learned about Tom Matthews and put to her the nagging question in the back of his mind. "Marilyn, to what extent does my Christian responsibility demand that I share my own defeats with other people, especially if this kind of openness could give someone else the courage to share their burdens as well?"

Marilyn responded slowly but firmly. "If you're thinking

about telling the world about being fired, that's nothing but masochism. You feel guilty about not having known about Tom Matthews. Maybe you *could* have helped him, but it's too late now. You would only be punishing yourself and your family by flaunting your failure. You've been one of the strongest leaders in forming the church koinonia groups. You've told me yourself that the sharing in this encounter group has been helpful for you and that you've really been able to give support to other people. You haven't felt you had to tell anyone in the group about the job thing and that's pretty clear evidence that you don't have to bare your soul to help someone else. Look, we live in a very status-conscious community and I don't want to have to deal with anyone else's pity."

Carl admitted that Marilyn hit some pretty raw nerves with that "status-conscious" comment. Marilyn's salary was small. He was already feeling the burden of the financial crunch if they were to maintain anything near their present lifestyle. He had to get a job in the next two weeks or go into debt. The application forms for unemployment compensation were staring him in the face. From the viewpoint of those "upstanding taxpaying citizens" in his economic bracket, "people on unemployment compensation are shiftless 'bums' waiting in line for a handout." Perhaps most problematic of all, could he really accept and face what he saw as personal failure to the extent that he could admit this to his friends?

But Carl also responded to what he saw as the "other side of the coin" as he argued with both himself and his wife. "Marilyn, Tom's suicide has painfully forced me to recognize the tremendous unspoken needs of people around us. I've talked before about the little 'pigeonholes' we put ourselves into and the crying need to break out of this pattern. We look to different kinds of programs in the church to do this for us, but we're not really willing to *risk* ourselves to get to know each other. I want to be honest with myself and with other people about where I am, but I don't know what that means for you or the boys *or* me."

Carl Phillips Was Fired
Study Guide

The extended family of the church is another context in which we find models for decision-making and value formation. Immediate family and the church are areas that overlap in the case of Carl Phillips. How Carl Phillips relates his personal crisis to his church family may deeply affect his own life and the lives of others.

To the central virtue of love the Bible adds the notion of faith. Faith describes a relation of trust and confidence in God. Belief in the freedom God has granted us in Jesus Christ allows us to be related to God in a new way and, consequently, related to our neighbor with trust. We can dare to risk sharing part of who we are with our neighbor, because of our faith in God's gift of support and new life. But the truth is that we don't always trust our neighbor and are not always trustworthy. This section will explore some guidelines for trusting to complement the guidelines for loving. The full potential of love may depend on being both trusting and trustworthy.

I. *The Basis of Trust*

Who does Carl Phillips trust? Carl did not share his loss of the job with his wife Marilyn, his sons, or his church koinonia group. Why? How do you think each of these "family members" do or will feel about Carl's withholding the information about being "phased out": anger, hurt, relief, frustration, care, concern?

What kind of model is Carl providing for Marilyn and his sons? Has Marilyn done anything that seems to justify Carl's initial decision? Do you think the boys will appreciate their parents' desire to protect them? How might you respond in their shoes?

II. *The Criteria of Human Worth*

Marilyn urges Carl not to flaunt his failure. What criteria do Carl and many other male heads of households seem to have for success or failure? What messages has this "status-conscious community" conveyed to Carl (production, prestige, money, etc.)? Where does Marilyn appear to find her sense of identity and worth? Does the Christian community confirm this list of criteria or are there alternative criteria for human worth? Do relationships count as much as production, "being" as much as "doing"? In this context how would you interpret the biblical text: "Greater love has no man than this, that a man lay down his life for his friends"? (John 15:13)

III. *Developing Trust*

The discussion leader could consider introducing a group roleplay in which the participants in the discussion play themselves as members of the koinonia group and the discussion leader assumes the role of Carl Phillips. Imagine the group has discovered, without Carl's knowledge, that he has lost his job and must decide how to respond as he convenes this evening meeting by saying, "What's on your minds tonight?" This may provide the opportunity to explore alternatives realistically. After the roleplay is concluded, the group could explore such questions as: Should they have confronted Carl directly or allowed him to share in his own time? If he does come to the group, what action might they recommend to him? Could or should the group contact Marilyn or the children? How can this extended family demonstrate trust of and love for Carl?

IV. *Locations of Grace*

What resources could the Phillips family or the koinonia group turn to whether or not Carl decides this is the appropriate time to share his problem? How can the biblical idea of bearing one another's burden, of weeping with those who weep and rejoicing with those who rejoice (Rom. 12:15) be applied, if at all? Where might healing and renewal occur? What would you pray for as a member of the koinonia group? How can the church contribute to guidelines for trusting based on faith in Jesus Christ as the one who heals, renews, and gives worth? One case discussion included in Guidelines for Trusting:

      Openness
      Vulnerability
      Confession
      Loyalty
      Confidence in Christ's Grace
Your group may wish to consider their own list to be used for the following cases in this section and to inform their own modeling.

V. *Use of the Case*

The essay on the "Case Method and Christian Living" might be read by a group as an introduction to this section on value formation in the church.

The case of Carl Phillips has proven to be a good discussion catalyst for adult education classes, men's and women's organizations, and family conferences or youth retreats where the role and feelings of the two sons is given special attention.

VI. *A Personal Footnote*

"Carl Phillips Was Fired" is, of course, disguised by new names and location to protect the privacy of the actual persons. The case was offered by Carl himself to aid other Christians, but his conversation originally focused on the plight of Mary Matthews, the widow of the friend who had committed suicide. Only in Carl's sharing during the interview did it become apparent that the more compelling case was not about Mary Matthews but about Carl himself. After reading the finished text, Carl proposed that the case be taught to the adult education seminar which he chaired in his own church. Carl hoped that the discussion of the disguised case in the midst of a class on Christian vocation, which involved some members of the koinonia group, might lead to greater insight for himself and for the class. The obstacle, beyond Carl's vulnerability, was the unknown risk to Mary Matthews who occasionally attended the class. To protect Mary's integrity, the case author and teacher decided, at Carl's suggestion, to bring an alternative case if Mary should be present.

The Sunday morning arrived and a nod from Carl indicated

that Mary was not there. The instructor began to lead the discussion, noting among other factors the guilt and despair of Mary Matthews over her husband's suicide. While writing a contributor's ideas on the board, the case instructor did not see one woman arrive late and slip into the back of the class. The teacher noticed how pale Carl was, but thought that a result of his discomfort over the analysis of his own case. After a very lively discussion hour, one of the class participants came to the instructor to introduce herself. Only then did the teacher realize that this was the real "Mary Matthews" of the morning's case. "You know," she declared, "this could have been my own case! It is identical to the tragedy of my own husband's death by suicide a few months ago." The case teacher was deeply concerned as he looked at her tear streaked face. "And I must confess," she continued, "this discussion is the most helpful thing that has happened to me since he died!"

The learning for the instructor was not to underestimate the healing and reconciling power of honest dialogue in which the Spirit's presence could allow Mary to find a new kind of wisdom about herself, and trust for other members of the Christian family. With growing maturity she may be better able to accept responsibility for decisions she must make about the past and the future. Mary found a resource of grace in those in her community and perceived the depth of their commitment to ministry to her and others caught in Tom Matthews' dilemma.

The guidelines for trusting were also clarified for Carl and the case writers in the experience of preparing, teaching, and evaluating Carl's own case in Christian living.

VII. *Suggested Additional Reading*

Richard Nelson Bolles, *What Color Is Your Parachute: A Practical Manual for Job Hunters & Career Changers* (Berkeley: Ten Speed Press), 1972, paperback; Michael Maccoby, *The Gamesman* (New York: Simon & Schuster), 1976; and Hendrik van Oyen, *Affluence and the Christian* (Philadelphia: Fortress Press), 1966, paperback.

A Youth Elder for Oak Brook

When Anne Hendricks left Pastor Sid Johnson's office in Oak Brook Community Church on Monday afternoon, he acknowledged that he was in the midst of a church-wide disagreement as well as a painful family dispute. Anne was a long-standing, active member of the Oak Brook Church. Along with several other members of the congregation, she was strongly opposed to the nomination of a 16-year-old young man to the church board of elders. On the other hand, Anne's sister Sue Link and Sue's husband, a pediatrician in the community—a couple also quite active in the church and community—were two of the more outspoken members in support of Bob Campbell's nomination. Bob had been nominated two weeks ago to fill one of the five vacancies on a ruling board of fifteen persons.

Sue Link had stated her position very clearly after church on Sunday. Oak Brook was presently a church of 900 members; more than 160 of those members were teenagers. Sue expressed a real concern that this was a group of young people from whom the congregation could learn and who needed a representative voice in the decision-making process of the church. After hearing some of the dissention about Bob Campbell's nomination, Sue had responded, "Bob was confirmed at fourteen and became a full member of our church at that time. He wasn't nominated just because the committee felt we needed a teenager, but because he is an outstanding young man. He is responsible and articulate. I have confidence in his judgment and feel there is no theological reason for us to assume that the Holy Spirit can't speak through him as well as through those of us with a few more years!"

Of Sue's four children two were in their teens, and both were active in the Oak Brook Youth Association. This was a church-related but community-wide group of about forty teenagers, over half of whom were "unchurched." They met weekly for study, worship, service projects, and recreation. Sue and her husband Tom were two of the parent leaders of this group. Both Sue and Tom had also been quite active in their concern for social issues in the community. Sue had in the past been an

elected elder in the congregation, presently taught a church
school class, was a popular Girl Scout troop leader, and voca-
tionally was a part-time guidance counselor in one of the area
high schools.

Though Sue Link and Anne Hendricks were fairly close as
sisters, Sid Johnson saw Anne's family style and understanding
of the church as quite different from Sue's. Sue was talented
artistically and had contributed beautiful contemporary ban-
ners for the sanctuary. She was presently in a new team teaching situation in the church and Sid characterized her as being
"in touch with the new life in the church." For twenty one years
Anne had been a farmer's wife and was the mother of six children. Sid smiled when he thought of the Hendricks family in
church each Sunday morning in the same pew. The girls, who
ranged in age from three to eighteen, wore braids and pressed
dresses; the boys, seven and fourteen, wore ties. The family
always sat together. Quite a contrast to the jean-clad youngsters
of the Links who were often dotted throughout the congregation.

Anne and her husband Fred were politically conservative.
Sid saw them as extremely honest, hard working people who
kept a firm rein on their children. Anne and Fred had not
permitted either of the older Hendricks girls or the teenage boy
to become members of the Oak Brook Youth Association.

In Sid's office on Monday afternoon Anne had spoken quite
strongly of her opposition, not to Bob Campbell personally, but
to the concept of a youth elder. "Sid, there have been many
changes in the church since you came six years ago. I know I
have been hesitant about some and supported others. I see the
church growing possibly as a result of some of these changes.
But I feel the idea of a person as young as sixteen being elected
as a ruling leader of this church is not sound. I realize there are
a few congregations where this has occurred in other states, but
that doesn't mean we have to do the same. Ours is one of the
most historic churches in New York State—over two hundred
years old. I think such a step away from the patterns of the past
is going too far toward destroying some of the fundamental
traditions of our church which have intrinsic value. The office

of elder places a tremendous responsibility on a person. My understanding of an 'elder' is someone who has not only a mature faith, wisdom, and dignity, but who can command the respect of the congregation. I don't think a teenager can fill those requirements. Furthermore, I am convinced that the election of Bob Campbell would be illegal. Sid, you know that a number of us have formed an ad hoc committee. We're going to do all we can to prevent that election."

With those words Anne had left Sid Johnson's office. Her final comment about the "legality" of Bob's election was one of the issues around which much of the controversy had become focused and the one in which Sue and Anne's father, Thomas Lawrence, had been quite outspoken.

Mr. Lawrence, one of the most respected members of the Oak Brook community, was a retired business executive who over the past forty years had assumed a strong leadership role in the church and in civic organizations. He had remained silent during the first week following the announcement of elder nominations two weeks before. However, now more than a week ago on the previous Sunday, he stated that though he "had no objection to the idea of a youth elder in theory" he objected on legal grounds. The church ruling board was "unicameral," meaning that the fifteen members not only made decisions of church policy but were empowered to make binding legal agreements for the congregation. Mr. Lawrence's lawyer had said that New York State Corporate law clearly stated that voting board members of any corporation must be twenty one years of age or older. Thus the financial position of all members of such an illegally composed board was endangered as they became personally liable for any financial commitments made by that board. Mr. Lawrence, who had served a number of times in the past on the ruling board, had also been one of the five persons nominated for the current slate. He had now withdrawn his name from that slate.

Earlier, Sid had done a good bit of research on the issue and had found no reasons in their church government against a youth elder. He then counseled with a member of the congregation who was a lawyer. She had said that the legal issue was purely a matter of interpretation and that she saw no basic conflict. When binding legal or financial votes on issues came before the board, which was really fairly seldom, Bob Campbell would simply abstain from voting and the majority of those voting would clearly constitute a quorum. Sid felt then that the legal issue was genuinely "a matter of interpretation."

Following the emergence of the legal issue, Sid had expressed a particular concern to be in touch with the feelings of the congregation on the whole matter. In the church bulletin, which came out weekly, there had been an announcement of the five nominees as well as statements of support for the various candidates. The following week Sid had agreed to print in the bulletin a statement from those opposed to the youth elder and the nomination by this group of an opposition candidate. This was published with the consent of Bob Campbell and his parents.

Sid Johnson had spoken with Bob and his family prior to Bob's accepting the nomination. Later, when opposition became clearly evident, Sid again counseled with the Campbell family. He indicated that he had had no idea the issue would become so involved and he wanted to assure Bob that he *personally* was not being opposed. Sid stated that he in no way wanted Bob to become the innocent victim of a church dispute. At this point Bob had responded to the issue. "Pastor Johnson, I have considered dropping my name from the list, but I really feel that I could do a good job of representing the younger people in the congregation. There are a lot of concerns we feel should be before the church. But I believe that those people who oppose the idea of a youth elder should definitely be given a voice in the church newsletter. This is an elected office in the church and I would much rather the whole thing be discussed above board. I don't think the congregation could ever feel any confidence in me unless my nomination is accepted openly."

Sid Johnson felt that he must be as open with the congregation as he was asking them to be with him. On Sunday following the appearance of the "opposition" newsletter Sid preached strongly in favor of Bob Campbell's election. He used as his basic text the Scripture from 1 Samuel 16: 1–13: "Man looks on

the outward appearance, but the LORD looks on the heart."
Sid's major point centered around the theme that "the measure
of the church is not in its changelessness but in its vitality." It
was on Monday following Sid's sermon that Anne Hendricks
had come to his office.

Monday evening Sid conferred with John Moore, the president of the church board and a close friend. John had publicly
expressed his support for a youth elder.

Sid was evaluating the congregational response to his sermon. "I think that people were in favor of both the sermon and
my intent, but I did meet with some pretty strong opposition.
One member said he felt I was using the pulpit unfairly, that
I was 'using my trump card to get my point across.'

"I somehow feel that this legal issue is more of a smoke
screen covering the basic problem. Anne and her father are in
some ways representative of a number of those who oppose Bob
Campbell. I appreciate and support the fact that for many of
these folks there are very real values in the security and stability
of the traditions in our church. The style of our worship in Oak
Brook Church has become much more informal in the past few
years; there are often guitars in the service, and openly verbal-
ized prayer requests from the congregation. It has become
more difficult to remain anonymous. There can be some real
threats involved with facing what I believe are the implications
of the gospel for the twentieth century. But it's very difficult for
many people to change their style of worship. I feel a real
responsibility to reach out to those who aren't with us and never
to shove them aside.

"I'm not absolutely certain how the vote will go, but I have
a pretty good idea that the congregation will vote strongly in
favor of Bob Campbell. At this point my major concern is ex-
pressing personal support for those who are in opposition. In
the past week I have had lunch with several in the congregation
who oppose Bob. We've tried to be open about this issue of a
youth elder and not set the church up for a covert split. But
some of our brothers and sisters seem absolutely locked into
their position.

"John, how can we conduct that meeting tomorrow night

and lovingly support those who are in opposition but at the same time maintain our own integrity on the issue?"

Youth Elder for Oak Brook
Study Guide

There are many different themes this case discussion could follow: use of pastoral authority; styles of parenting; conflict management; definition of "elder"; images of youth; etc. Following our Guidelines for Trusting, one pattern may be to focus on *change* and *models.*

How do we in the church, which claims to have a change-less gospel, deal with change? Many Christians feel that the history and traditions of the church provide an extremely important foundation for our faith. The adherance to certain creeds has sought to keep the church faithful to the New Testament intent. There is also a very positive sense of security derived from following established patterns. Psychologists indicate that consistent patterns of family life are crucial to a child's growth and development. The same could be true for members of the Christian family. Yet Christ has called us to put new wine into fresh wine skins (Matt. 9:17). New knowledge and insights often necessitate our growing and changing, whereas we can become bound by the old patterns. These changes can also be very threatening. How can one be supported by the foundations of faith, yet free to seek new ways of expression? How can we judge when changes must be made? What are the necessary elements for creative change to occur? How important is *trust* in the process of change?

The Goals of Congregational Life, the qualities we seek to model, have been discussed as Wisdom, Maturity, and Discernment. These values seem particularly important as members of the Oak Brook family select new congregational leaders. A significant focus for this case could be on the meaning of these values, particularly maturity. What does maturity have to do with age and experience? Can you trust someone who is not mature? Are there levels of trusting and maturity? Paul calls on

Timothy to "Let no one despise your youth, but set the believers an example in speech and conduct, in love, in faith, in purity." (1 Timothy 4:12). Paul is asking Timothy to be a model for other Christians. What are some of the criteria for Christian maturity?

I. *The Influence of Models*

A. One way to begin case discussion may be to focus on the *families* of Sue Link and Anne Hendricks. Both styles of parenting may be good, but they are clearly different. What do you think each mother *expects* of her children? One's expectations are usually guided by a model. What images or models for teens does each mother have? Comments from this discussion might be listed on the board for clarity and contrast.

Discuss how your image of another may affect your attitude toward that person. How does your attitude about a person affect his/her behavior? Can you trust someone you do not respect? In turn, does trust affect one's ability to mature?

B. In this case it is clear that there are different images or models for an "elder." Discuss and list the models for Sue, Anne, Sid Johnson, and Bob Campbell. Do you have any indication what Thomas Lawrence's model for an elder would be? How seriously do you take the issue of legality? Why might it be difficult for Anne Hendricks to combine her model for an elder and her image of a teen? Do you agree with Sid that Anne is threatened by the changes in the church? Has Sid Johnson's sermon jeopardized or strengthened the trust of his congregation?

C. How does *your* own image of young people and your model for a church leader affect your viewpoint in this case?

Consider placing the entire discussion group in a roleplay situation. Let them become the Oak Brook congregation as it is called to discuss and vote on the new elders. The members of the group should play *themselves* and voice their own opinions as they imagine they are members of Oak Brook. The pastor, perhaps played by the discussion leader, could moderate the meeting.

The moderator should be aware of the things learned so far

in the discussion and consider how he or she can most constructively conduct the meeting keeping in mind the Guidelines for
Trusting. Are Bob Campbell and the other nominees present or
excused? You might begin with statements of support for Bob
Campbell and the opposition nominee. The moderator might
list key points on the board.

II. *Resources of Grace*

A. After a roleplay of 10–15 minutes the group may want
to adjourn the meeting and consider what occurred. Could the
meeting have been organized or conducted in a different way?
What preparation for this congregational meeting was necessary? You might also discuss how you could resolve any conflict
in the congregation. Can open conflict be a creative force? Why
or why not? Has your group learned anything from one another?

B. How can members of a congregation love and support
one another in the midst of change and conflict? How can you
continue to trust someone with whom you are in conflict? Discuss what the class sees as resources of grace, creative avenues
for reconciling the situation in Oak Brook Church or in their
own "congregational meeting."

III. *Use of the Case*

This case has been used effectively in officer training sessions to focus on the nature of the church, in a pastors' conference on the role and responsible use of pastoral authority, in
youth groups, and in a congregational meeting for a church
dealing with changing liturgy.

IV. *Suggested Additional Reading*

Dietrich Bonhoeffer, *Life Together* (New York: Harper &
Row), 1976, paperback; Robert M. Brown, *The Significance of
the Church* (Philadelphia: Westminster Press), 1956, paperback; and Robert A. Evans and Thomas D. Parkers, eds., *Christian Theology: A Case Method Approach* (New York: Harper &
Row), 1976. See section 7, pp. 189–212.

Pray for a Miracle

Don Jacobs rang the doorbell, hesitantly. He knew Aunt Alice would answer in a minute. He could almost picture her coming from Alfred's bed through the hall toward the living room. He also knew what she would soon be asking him. "Pray for a miracle." Somehow that phrase stuck with her, from an evangelist or something.

Don wondered again how to respond. If he did what she asked he would feel like a hypocrite of sorts. But if he denied her request he would undoubtedly disappoint her. He tried to gather confused thoughts as the encounter drew nearer.

Aunt Alice and Uncle Alfred

For 42 of their 56 years of marriage, Alice and Alfred had been living right here on Sycamore Street. The clapboard house, now with its porch a bit askew, had been only a few years old when they moved in. They used to tell Don how small the neighborhood trees had been in those days. Now trees almost overlapped the street, and the sidewalks cracked with the pressure of the big roots.

Together Alice and Alfred had shared work, a small grocery, and they had shared play, especially the good times with the family. They had been inseparable as Alice recounted it and as Don remembered. Seldom had either gone out alone, except to night meetings of Alfred's service club or sometimes to church. Alice had told Don, with tears in her eyes, just last week: "You see that bed Alfred is in? Until his illness, we had been together in that bed every night for two decades. We took some trips before that, but Alfred has never been away from me overnight."

Both Alice and Alfred were Christians. She had worked in Women's Guild and he as a deacon as long as Don had known them. Alice read the family Bible a lot now, and Don remembered her taking it out each Saturday night when he had been with them.

Don Jacobs

Don's own parents had died when he was eight. He had lived almost ten years with Alice and Alfred. Then he went off to college, and yet they kept in touch with him as though they were his real parents. Don had known other family members, cousins and such, through Alice and Alfred. And the bond had stayed a close one through the years. Don had married and he lived with his family about twenty miles away. His kids considered Alice and Alfred as grandparents, and they lavished affection on all the Jacobs.

Don's own theology had changed over time. He had grown to think of prayer as important and as personally helpful. One prayed to be "in touch" with God, not to get anything to happen. He had read, among other works, a remarkable thing by Mark Twain about prayer. Mark Twain had made fun of selfish prayers, something about God responding to one man's request by saying a competitor prayed the opposite and the two prayers cancelled each other out. That had made an impression on Don.

Yet he prayed. Sometimes he even repeated a word or two, in order to concentrate. He did not ask for things, though. After all, if God knew everything what was the use? Mostly Jacobs prayed "to get his life in focus" by pushing out all other things from his mind. That left a beautiful void that concentrated his energy afterwards on the task at hand, or on the needs of others. Don could not help but feel a bit suspicious of the evangelists who offered "good results" from prayer, a kind of manipulation of things in favor of the contributor. And he believed in the possibility of some kind of life after death, though he hoped natural events would not be absent there—wherever "there" was. As a scientist he felt strongly about the interdependence of all natural processes, and the beauty of nature appealed to him in a religious fashion.

Alfred's Illness

Uncle Alfred was now almost seventy-two as Don remembered the dates. He had lived a really full life, quietly and with dignity. About three years ago he had been diagnosed as needing surgery. Cancer had been discovered, and gradually evi-

dence of brain cancer had appeared. Alfred had been hospital-
ized from time to time, then allowed to "recuperate" at home
whenever possible. His condition had deteriorated over the
months of illness, so that recently he had been lucid only rarely.
When he woke up, Alfred would begin to cry uncontrollably.
He would seldom recognize anybody, Alice included. Mostly he
just lay there, dying.

His weight had decreased over the months until he was just
"skin and bones," as Alice described him. Other symptoms indicated that he would soon pass away, and the doctors had
advised that Alice should place him in the hospital for an easier
time of it.

Alice's Care and Prayer

Alice long ago had received some training as a nurse's aid.
She wanted to care for Alfred as much as possible at home,
"where things were familiar."

For the operations, she had stayed constantly at the hospital. At home she stayed right by his side almost all the time. Of
late, she had been requesting all the persons visiting to "pray
for a miracle." Rev. Wilkins had been there two days ago, and
he had prayed about "God's will be done. . . ." Don had thought
the prayer a good one, but after Rev. Wilkins left Alice confided
that she did not think that was enough. "He said that God's will
be done to heal or bring Alfred to Himself," Alice related. "I
know Alfred can be restored to useful health. God will do it if
our faith is strong enough."

Don tried to go to see them daily, either at lunch or in the
evening. Yesterday Alice had become more insistent. "Pray for
him, Donald. You're a good Christian man. God will listen to
you." Don had prayed something like this, as he recalled:

> God, who makes and redeems each of us, we seek your
> presence with Alfred. Care for him, God, because we
> surely do. Be with him and help him. Help us too, God,
> for we need your love and care. Amen.

Don had tried to let that be that, but as he left Alice had
said something about "a miracle." It was a fixation with her
right now. Don felt that he didn't even know what "restored to

health" meant for Alfred. He felt that Alice was focusing on
something that would not be helpful in her grief. But what to
do about it? What should he do?

Pray for a Miracle
Study Guide

In many of the earlier case discussions a consistently suggested "resource of grace" has been prayer. This medium of
communication with God is central to our vision of Christian
living. It is a process, however, that is understood by Christians
in many different and often conflicting ways. Christ declared
that "whatever you ask in prayer, you will receive, if you have
faith" (Matt. 22), yet Jesus' own example in prayer was to ask
"not as I will, but as thou wilt" (Matt. 26:39). These two guidelines for prayer seem to involve different kinds of trust. An open
discussion of "Pray for a Miracle" may help clarify your own
concept of trust in God and your understanding of prayer.

I. *The Nature of Prayer*

Your discussion might begin by asking members of the
group if they could say in one sentence what Don might responsibly pray for. When these responses are listed, does any pattern
develop that suggests what the group thinks prayer involves?
Does the Lord's Prayer give any guidance in form or content?
How might Don's prayer reflect trust in God? Would his prayer
demonstrate a trusting relationship to his aunt and other members of his extended family? How do your own guidelines for
trusting inform your understanding of the nature of prayer?

Experience with the case indicates that other concerns also
emerge.

II. *Personal Integrity*

Can Don Jacobs remain true to himself while also trying to
please Aunt Alice and help her? The interplay of internal and
external expectations in the matter of integrity is very important. How do you deal with conflicting expectations and keep
your integrity?

III. *Helping People*

As several of the introductory essays attest, Christian values include sharing at the very core of life. Models for Don Jacobs include the actions of Aunt Alice and Uncle Alfred in his own life. They had given of themselves in his need, and now he is attempting to come to terms with Alice's request and needs. Should Don share his concerns with Aunt Alice? If so, how might that be done in the most loving and trusting way?

IV. *Religious Language*

Every word is a symbol, and religious words most of all are not able to convey all the richness of religious experience. "I believe in God the Father almighty, maker of heaven and earth. . . ." When we say the Creed, we are not just voicing simple words about reality: we are also standing with millions of Christian people over the centuries to repeat their statements of meaning and life. The same is true with the words of prayer— how inadequate all prayer words are! Paul even said the "Spirit intercedes for us with a sigh. . . ." What language do you use in prayer? What name do you give to God—Father, Shepherd, Lord? What does this say about what you expect or about your relationship to God? Are the words or symbols of prayer different when you do Bible study or discuss the needs of a friend?

V. *Miracles and Resources of Grace*

One other matter might come up, and hopefully your group will learn by discussing it—the matter of miracles. Throughout the nineteenth century Christians concerned themselves perhaps too much with the meaning of miracles, and whether God works in nature or defies nature with special acts. Today, however, the dialogue does not occur very often. Christian life is lived very much according to the ways we see God working in the world. Therefore people should be encouraged to form their understanding of God's actions—whether they consider miracles a part of that activity or not. Leaders might remember that conscientious Christians have taken both sides of the nineteenth century argument about miracles, that the Christian family includes many points of view, and that

people grow in learning from each other. Would Don pray for
a miracle? What would that mean if he did?

VI. *Bridging Exercise*

One exercise that has proven helpful in some groups is to
ask the participants who decide Don should make a prayer,
"What would you pray?" As already indicated, directions such
as this one would be invitations to take part instead of orders
to "Write a prayer." This exercise may bring the group back to
the opening discussion and be a form of summary. Also it could
be a project for another session to explore further the meaning
of prayer. Other resources to be drawn on might be your pastor
or the introductory essay on "Christian Living in the Early
Church." A basic consideration could be whether or not prayer
is essential to the rhythm of the life of the church that encourages trust in God and neighbor.

VII. *Suggested Additional Reading*

Do not be afraid of relating this situation to your own experience and to the experiences of members of the group. Some
books that can help include: Jacques Ellul, *Prayer and Modern
Man* (New York: Seabury), 1970; George Buttrick, *Prayer*
(Nashville: Abingdon), 1942; Mac and Anne Turnage, *The Mystery of Prayer* (Richmond: John Knox Press), 1964; Annette
Walthus, *Prayer—Who Needs It?* (Camden, N.J.: Thomas Nelson, Inc.), 1970.

5 / The Society: Guidelines for Responding

The Thomas Family Goes Private

"Bob has made up his mind. Grace and Lindsey are going to Evangel Preparation Academy, and that's that unless I really fight him about it. Lord knows what will happen if I disagree! Busing is a terrible thing, but so is ghetto education. I have been around the black schools long enough to see that integration is the only way for this to be stopped. But when it comes to the subjecting of our own kids to abuse and other things like that, I get all unsure. To buck Bob at this point, I would have to be dead certain, I think; and that is not the case at all. I have listened to the kids, and I do know what they want—they want to stay in North High. I also have a sneaking suspicion they are the ones who know best about their own education. But Bob has put his foot down."

Millie Thomas spoke with evident feeling. Even when she digressed from the problem at hand—her husband's decision to take the two younger children (going into the 10th and 7th grades, respectively) from public schools because of court-ordered integration—she was very obviously grieved at the lack of communication with her husband on the subject. Sporadically she would cease to speak and simply sob quietly. Mourning did not become her, for ordinarily Millie seemed full of vitality and she appeared to hold a rather "sunny view" of the universe in general. She moved from the general to the specific in her recounting of the history of their interaction.

"Here in Dunlap, integration had not progressed very far since the Supreme Court decision of 1954. Yes, we had a few mixed schools under a freedom of choice plan in the middle sixties, but they were middle class blacks moving into white schools. North High itself was all white, running all the way from the first to the twelfth grades. The school had been built in the early fifties as an experiment in mixing lower and upper grades for a sense of educational continuity. We looked around when we moved here in 1962 and Bob, Jr., was just starting school. Everything looked perfect and we bought not three blocks away. Bob, Jr., has gone straight through North High and the others are following suit—or at least were.

"The order to start busing came during the summer before last. About 35% of the students at North would be bused to Liston School if elementary and to Central if in high school. A corresponding number of black children would come from Liston and from Central to replace them. I told the family we should be thankful that we beat the odds, because all three children got to stay here. During the fall, nothing spectacular happened. Lindsey did have a black teacher, but Miss Morris (that was her name) was better than the other sixth grade teachers, and everyone knew it. Several of our neighbors decided to move to the country, and they sold their homes and moved out. But we never even thought about it. Bob did say he hoped whites bought the houses, but I thought nothing of that kind of remark.

"The problem started for us when Grace was assaulted physically. It was truthfully the only major problem of the year. I do not mean to say it was a little thing at all. Her eye was swollen for three days. It seems she was leaving gym class, when she stumbled into another girl—a black girl. Immediately the black girl pushed her back and accused her of intentionally trying to shove her so she would fall. Grace tried to explain; but before she could get out even some of the words, this girl and some friends began to hit and kick her. Grace said the gym teacher, who is black, tried to break it up and succeeded with the help of some other people, both black and white. But they did give Grace a black eye. I mean it was discolored some.

"Bob said something like, 'That settles it!' at the time, when Grace came home that night. We all talked about the difficulties that people have when they try to bridge gaps. Honestly I thought we had just passed through an unpleasant experience. Grace seemed to forget it during the spring, tried out for the *North Poll* (the school newspaper), and dated several different boys.

"Then just last week, a full two months after the incident and only a week before school let out, Bob told us he had decided that Grace and Lindsey would be better off in the Evangel Academy next year. He said he spoke with Sherman Boehms, who was organizing the new school, and it was all settled. Bob, Jr., could stay at North because 'he could take care of himself.' Tuition for Grace and Lindsey would be $1,100 together since they could discount a second child. And that was the way it would be."

Evangel Preparation Academy was one of the new schools opening in the metropolitan Dunlap area in response to court ordered busing. It promised to have qualified teachers, a $650 tuition, and students from grades 1–10. The Academy did not yet have a building of its own, but would use the spacious facilities of the Simple Faith Church of Christ and construct eventually on an adjacent lot. Already a number of parents promised support of the Academy, although Dr. Boehms would not give specific figures to outsiders on their enrollment.

"At times of crisis, Bob kind of turns inward. We had all prayed together at supper the night Grace got hurt, but from that time on he just took it all on his shoulders. When he announced his decision, there was no room for alternatives. In his mind, the case was closed.

"I remember when we moved to Dunlap. Bob had gotten the offer from United Furniture, and he talked with me about the fact that he would have to travel some if he accepted. Then, a week or so later he just came home and said 'I've accepted it.' We had the two young ones and the third was almost here. Probably I should have been more vocal about my feelings, but off we went. On the other hand, he has not fussed at all about my going back to work. I know we can use the money, with Bob, Jr., so close to college and the other two not far behind. But we do not really need it. I work more because I like to than that

I have to. Counseling the juveniles is fulfilling. It is a challenge and I think I can help them. Bob is great about that, just as he was about my doing all that volunteer work for the church.

"I have been more socially sensitive since we began the church tutorial program than Bob has ever been. Come to think of it, I am not really certain he understands all the implications of the decision to move the children to the private school. Not only does it have an effect on us, it will also mean fewer state funds for the system. Most of all, it's the future of the kids I think about. They are not set for a full educational program at Evangel. And the children want to stay at North in spite of the trouble.

"Speaking of trouble, there is bound to be more next year at North. With some whites withdrawing the racial balance might even change. Then we see the courts being so indecisive, and we are uncertain what the next decision will be.

"I went to my minister, who is also a good friend. He was sympathetic but said after we prayed about it that I should stick by Bob's thinking. He told me about a couple that are separated because of the wife taking a stronger position on something than she used to. I love Bob dearly, and would not think of divorce. I am confident of his love for me, too.

The Thomas Family Goes Private
Study Guide

Remember the story of the lighthouse keeper whose lighthouse worked on coal oil? A friend on the island dropped by, and asked to borrow a little oil for a lamp at home. Then another . . . another . . . another. To each the lighthouse keeper replied, "Sure, there's bound to be a lot for such a big light as this, and you just want a little. Here." After many friends had come, a storm arose. The lighthouse keeper tried to start the light to warn an approaching boat about the shoal nearby. But there was no oil left. The light remained unlit, and the boat crashed on the rocks.

The lesson in the story was apparent: "Don't whittle away

on resources; concentrate on things that count and perform your responsibility when the time comes." In sermons the story is often linked with Jesus' parable of the "wise and foolish maidens" (Matthew 25:1–13).

On the other hand, Jesus also told about the "good Samaritan" (Luke 10:29–37), the epitome of caring in a human situation. This man risked his life in helping a victim of robbers, spending his resources without counting costs upon a person who was not even a friend. Sharing for the good Samaritan meant thinking first of another person, being a servant of others.

Both these parables suggest guidelines for responding to situations, and in the world we sometimes act responsibly by following either precept. However, there is a tension between these two. They appear to be exactly opposite, yet both are valid and both are avenues of caring. Guidelines for Responding must account for both responsible stewardship of God's gifts and sacrificial giving. Decisions about sharing and about responding are the particular concerns of these next three cases. In each case the distinct pressures from the society we live in affect the decision-making and value formation of a family.

In the first case, "The Thomas Family Goes Private," your concern may well be on the busing situation in which they are involved. Again, it may focus on the communication and interpersonal problems within the Thomas family. Whatever center you find for your discussion, consider the responsibility of Millie Thomas as a Christian person and the sharing that is desperately needed between the Thomas family, their congregation, and their community.

I. *Responsible Alternatives*

One way to begin case discussion is to ask about Millie's alternatives. What can she do? What factors must be considered in any decision? You can move from that analysis to one of the ethical choice Millie should make. How is Millie's integrity involved? What are the social and Christian implications of her choices?

II. *Priorities in Responding*

Who is my neighbor, and what are the boundaries of my responsibility? In communities directly affected by court orders to integrate schools, perhaps no issue commands as much feeling as busing. Reasonable and constructive discussions on the subject are sometimes difficult even in churches (sometimes difficult *especially* in churches). Most of the private schools opened in response to busing, at least in the communities of which we are aware, call themselves "Christian academies."

Such is the case with the Thomas family and "Evangel Preparation Academy." Most of these academies are all-white in enrollment and leadership. The nature and implications of such an understanding of Christian living may well occupy a part of your discussion. What can we learn about our own community from a study of this case? What about the use of "Christian" in segregated academies? Would the issues be different if we were talking about a good private secular school? Many who are in favor of private schooling for their children argue that their first responsibility is to offer the best possible education to their own children. They will insist it is an issue of quality and not of segregation. How would you respond?

If your group is itself integrated, your discussion will probably be most helpful. This has been our experience, thus far in the study of this case. However, if your group is all-black or all-white, you can still deal sensitively with this controversial issue of busing and the problems of the Thomas family. You probably will not achieve a consensus on the ethical way for Millie to proceed. Even as you disagree, you will hopefully be sharing together values, experiences, and insights that will be of mutual benefit.

III. *Changing Styles of Responding*

If busing is not a direct issue in your community, your consideration of the Thomas family will be more on the values they live, and how they embody (or fail to embody) Christian ways of relating to one another.

What models do Bob, Jr. and Lindsey have for relating to

the problems of their society? Should they have a role in the decision? If so, what should it be and why?

What is the nature and function of the minister, and the church, in this case? What does the minister, what does the church, mean to Millie? To Bob?

How were Bob's values formed? Can they change now? If so, how? Have Millie's values changed? Why or why not? How could Christian Guidelines for Responding apply to the members of the Thomas family?

IV. *Guidelines for Responding*

The essays on "Modeling as a Process" and "Parish Revitalization" may be a helpful accompaniment to a study of this case. Consider applying the "characteristics of a vital congregation" (p. 24) to the members of the Thomas family. This list may be helpful in developing your own Guidelines for Responding. Beyond being a catalyst for open discussion aimed directly at problems of church and society such as racism, this case has been used effectively in a women's group dealing with husband-wife relationships, and in an all-church family retreat.

V. *Suggested Additional Reading*

John M. Rich, ed., *Conflict and Decision* (New York: Harper & Row), 1972, especially chapters 2, 3, 4, and 6; John Howard Yoder, *The Politics of Jesus* (Grand Rapids: William B. Eerdmans), 1972.

Westport Grass

"Keeping her in is the least I can do. She'll run away if I do it. If I don't she'll just keep going to hell in a wheelbarrow."   Mrs. Katy James

"I swear I'll get the hell out of here and go to California. She thinks I'm a kid. I'm seventeen, for God's sake."   Linda James

Nancy Heiser knew when the 6:15 call came that Linda James was in trouble again. As a youth leader, she had known Linda as an obstinate member of the Y.P.F. (Young People's Fellowship) for two years.

"Mrs. Heiser? This is Katy James. Would you come right over?" Nancy said, "I have a meeting of the Y.P.C. (Council of the fellowship group). Could this wait until 9:30 or so, after the meeting?"

"No, my husband Ronald will be back about 10 and we need to get this thing settled. We need you now." Nancy called the president of the fellowship and told him to go ahead without her. "I'll get there when I can," she said.

Nancy drove the three miles to Westport Vista where the James family lived. She was trying to recall data about the family. They lived in a small apartment in Westport Village, the best suburb of town, so that Linda could attend Westport High School. The older children were in all kinds of trouble. Harry has been A.W.O.L. from Fort Dixon, and now was evidently an alcoholic somewhere nearby, because Linda spoke every once in a while about him. Willa, too, had been rather wild at Central High. A rumor circulated that she was arrested for prostitution during her senior year. Now Linda. . . .

Linda was a striking girl to look at, beautiful features, good figure, running for at least three years with an older crowd of kids. That's how she had first come to the youth group—with Jim Thatcher who was a senior at the time. Jim had graduated and went off to Beloit College, but Linda had kept coming off and on to the group. For one thing, Centenary Church had an excellent softball team, and Linda was a fine player. But Nancy suspected that Linda came mostly to be with the boys.

Sam, one of the fellows in the youth group, mentioned Linda's use of drugs first to Nancy, who had taken the initiative and asked Linda to eat out at the Pancake House after one game. That was more than a month ago. Nancy had gone ahead to make an offer of help at that time: "If you're on stuff and want off, we can get you help and your parents don't need to know about it."

Linda had responded with diffidence: "You're a gossip, and I don't need you."

Strangely enough, though, Linda had been conspicuous at church since then, with a whole month or more of regularity both at Y.P.F. and at morning worship.

As she arrived at the door Nancy could hear Linda yelling, "You won't keep me from anything!"

"Oh, come in, Mrs. Heiser. Thank you for coming." Mrs. James took Nancy's raincoat. Quickly Linda explained why the confrontation occurred: "Mother found some grass and pills in my drawer."

"Yes, I was putting some things away for Linda and saw it." Mrs. James offered.

"Holy ____, mother! It was all wrapped up in a bag. You had absolutely no right to look. I am entitled to my privacy. Don't you think so?"

"What did you do?" asked Nancy.

"My first thought was to show it to Ronald. He'd probably beat her and call the police too. But Ronald and I don't talk together much. With me working days and him working 'swing' we just don't. So I told Linda that she can't go out for two weeks —except to church and youth group, of course."

"And I told you I'll just leave!" Linda walked (or rather stalked) around the room.

Nancy wanted to shake some sense (or at least some calm) into Linda, but she attempted to settle her down by ignoring her and by speaking again to Mrs. James.

"Why did you think punishment like this would be the right thing?"

"Dr. Ayers was counseling Linda last year. She went several times to one of his groups, but quit because she said it was all girls. Anyway he said for me to keep her home as a punishment. That's something she doesn't like to do—stay home."

"Mommy's always doing what other people say," Linda chimed in. "That's the way it is right now. She doesn't give a ____ whether I pop stuff or not. Do you know what she said? She said, 'Linda, what will people think if you get arrested for using drugs?' "

"Where is the marijuana now?" asked Nancy.

"Oh," Mrs. James responded, "I put it back in her drawer, and the pills too."

"Let's get it out," Nancy decided and announced.

When they went together to the bedroom, Linda gesturing angrily that they should just leave her things alone, Mrs. James opened the drawer. She took out a rather large bag and handed it to Nancy quickly, wiped her hands in a rather loud, clapping motion, and said: "I sure am glad to hand this over to you."

Nancy opened the bag and discovered two parcels—one held several hundred red capsules, the other at least a pound of what looked like marijuana. "I had no idea you were talking about this much," she said.

"That's not much," Linda retorted. "Put it back."

Westport Grass
Study Guide

Society puts special pressures on the lives of some families and congregations. The freedom to both use and abuse intoxicating substances are examples of these pressures. How should a society responsibly control the use of drugs or alcohol? As we seek patterns for Christian living, how do we give preventive and therapeutic care for those persons who appear to abuse this freedom?

I. Ways to Respond

As Christian people, what responsibility do we have to intervene in the lives of others? And when are our actions inter-

ference in things that are not our business? Is it the invitation
that should prompt intervention? Does it have to be spoken in
words?

Biblical themes may be of help. Who receives the attention
of Jesus and his healing power? Is it only those who ask for it
directly like the blind beggar who called out to Jesus (Mark
10:46–52)? Or may family members or friends ask for help, as
the centurion did for his servant (Matt. 8:5–13) or as Mary and
Martha did for their brother Lazarus (John 11:1–44)?

II. *Responsibility and Action*

This case was generated during a course of study at a youth
retreat in which young people and adults sought to define "par-
ental" responsibility.

They pointed us to a situation that would offer material for
study. Since "Westport Grass" was constructed in response to
felt needs for study and guidance, let us share some ideas and
insights from one discussion.

Some questions by the leader that provoked learning:

What can you infer about Linda's relationship with her
mother, Katy James?

Were there surprises for Nancy Heiser as she got involved in the situation?

What should Nancy Heiser do now, at this point?

III. *Ways for Responding*

The young people and grownups involved in discussion of
this case had assigned themselves homework in preparation for
the session. Several of them brought material on drug abuse
that they considered pertinent for study.

One, for example, had been reading about "the drug epidemic." She sought to draw our attention to the importance of
recognizing needs for early prevention of serious problems. She
brought as evidence the statement by Ari Kiev, who worked
with addicts, that "early detection of fresh cases" of drug abuse
and quick initial treatment "constitute fundamental preventive
strategies."

Another participant had discovered a study showing definite correlation between drug abuse and usage of "safe" drugs,

like caffeine, nicotine in cigarettes, and alcohol. She wanted the case to tell more about Katy James' use of drugs and the other models for Linda. It was she who turned our attention to the fact that alcohol and cigarette nicotine are really number one problems of drug abuse in the U.S.

One of the young people was especially concerned about our stereotyping drug abusers. He told about his own experience at a party where conversation had assumed all drug users were "dope fiends."

Perhaps your learning will be along these lines, and homework assignments may be in order in addition to case reading. Here are some resources for you, available in nearby libraries and excellent on the matter of drug abuse.

Lloyd Johnson, *Drugs and American Youth* (Ann Arbor: Institute for Social Research), 1973. Here are results of a long term study of American teenagers from across the country over a four year period.

Ari Kiev, *The Drug Epidemic* (New York: The Free Press), 1975. A doctor speaks clearly about drug problems.

Norman Zinberg et al., *Drugs and the Public* (New York: Simon and Schuster), 1972. Here are some simply stated guides for helping drug abusers, along with all kinds of information on the various problems.

IV. *Playing Out the Future*

You might also want to use roleplay during the session itself. We have employed a technique called "role reversal" when youth and parents are together for this case. Ask a young person to become Mrs. Heiser, and another to be Mrs. James. Ask an adult to be Linda James. Then turn them loose with the question: "Where do you go from here (the end of the case)?" Let the three people act out what they would do, in roles, and let the other class members coach them if needed. Then talk about what went on and about responsibility for Christian living.

Some issues on which your discussion might focus are:

1. Mrs. Heiser may destroy any future relationship with Linda if she reports Linda's possession of drugs to the police, yet

she breaks the law if she does not. Discuss the implications of her decision. What Guidelines for Responding to Linda and her mother should she follow?

2. What does the existence of so much marijuana-looking stuff and so many pills in Linda's drawer mean? Is drug use itself contrary to Christian living? Why or why not?

3. Does Paul's language about glorifying God in your body (1 Corinthians 6:19–20) apply to this case? How does it relate to Paul's concern that Christians are free for all things but responsible for not causing a brother to stumble (1 Corinthians:8–9)?

V. *Use of the Case*

The use of "Westport Grass" for a Youth Retreat or with parents and young people has been mentioned. It may serve to raise the issue of the Christian's responsibility to the society and the just application of its laws. Since case studies may help in the clarification of these issues, the essay on "The Case Approach to Christian Living" might accompany a study of this case.

VI. *Suggested Additional Reading*

Frank Gannon, *Drugs: What They Are, How They Look, What They Do* (New York: Third Press), 1971; Jess Lair, *"I ain't much, baby—but I'm all I've got"* (Greenwich, Conn.: Fawcett), 1974, paperback.

Susan Carr's Decision

Driving home from her group at the Florence Nightingale Home, Susan Carr was conscious of her puzzlement over Ann Jones' situation. Susan had been counseling so many women lately. She felt satisfaction from the apparent success of her efforts. Still, she was troubled by this particular case. Should she counsel Ann to keep the baby? Should she listen with a view to Ann's putting the child up for adoption? Should she try to listen and refrain from influencing the decision at all?

Susan reviewed in her mind the situation as Ann had presented it to the group. Ann, a 26-year-old woman, had earned a B.S. in nursing and had worked five years. The second of five children, Ann had evidently been a responsible person, the caretaker of her younger brother and sisters. Ann had excelled in school, by all accounts, and she had spoken highly of her skills learned in college. Midwestern Wesleyan, where she took nursing, offered a good program mixing classroom time with actual experience in the Community Hospital. Ann, on scholarship, had maintained a job through college years as well.

Summing up her training, Ann had said at one point, "It was good, all right! I went to work straight out of school, in an intensive care unit. Folks at the school and the hospital, too, urged me to go get a master's degree and teach. I think that would be good."

Ann had spoken rather freely in the group of her relationship. "I really thought I was in love. Tim Wiggins was very kind, and gentle. And he gave me lots of attention. I guess that's why I fell for him.

"Oh, he had his faults too. He was sort of restless—never knew for sure what he wanted to do next. But I never let that bother me. I figured it was his business to find something he liked to do."

Susan remembered that members of the group listened attentively as Ann spoke. "I wasn't sure I should tell him I was pregnant. I didn't know what he would do. He was away for awhile so I just put off telling him. I was opposed to abortion. On religious grounds I just didn't think it was right for me. So

I really didn't consider having one. When Tim came back, I told him how I felt. He said whatever I wanted was O.K., but he never mentioned any concrete possibility of the two of us getting together. He kept coming by, but he didn't offer any commitment."

Ann had clenched her hands into fists, and her face had tightened noticeably. "I finally told Tim not to worry himself. I had decided on my own to have the baby. Right then I started figuring how I'd do it. Oh, I kept on seeing Tim, hoping somehow we might make it. But we never did.

"I made my own plans—called a friend here in Eastover who made arrangements for me to stay at Florence Nightingale. I kept saving my money and working at the hospital, as long as they would let me. That would give me at least something to live on. I even told my family.

"My parents refused to speak to me for awhile, but my aunt said I could stay with her after I leave here. My brothers and sisters are giving me lots of support. Now I need to make up my mind what to do. And I'm hoping you can help me, Susan. Should I keep the child, or sign the papers for adoption? I only have another week or so."

Reflecting on the exchanges and on Ann's story, Susan Carr realized that she was placed in a quandary. In this particular situation, what would be the best for Ann? Assuming that she would mostly listen, would her enthusiasm and bias be in favor of adoption? There were many families waiting to adopt a child. Adoptive families did have problems, but the baby would then have a mother and a father. Ann could then be freer to continue her education and career. Should she suggest that Ann keep the child? There were many single parent families raising children successfully. Ann certainly was a responsible person, and she had experience already with children. Whose baby was it, anyway? Susan asked herself.

Susan remembered Ann's smile as she had related her fantasy of keeping the baby and caring for it. But, weighing the consequences, she wondered if others whose support Ann needed would help her. Would she need the support of others?

Susan realized she could counsel as non-directively as possible, and provide Ann with information about adoption, single-parenting, and other issues. She was pondering her alternatives, not sure what to do.

Susan Carr's Decision
Study Guide

Counseling is an important form of responding. Christians, like all people, are giving and receiving counsel all the time. Some of you are involved more deeply in the formal arrangements for counseling, as are the two women in this case. Whether the counseling is informal or rigorous, there are several important questions for all participants.

How is listening related to the advice-giving on the part of the person giving counsel? On the other hand, how is the listening related to the decision-making on the part of the receiver of counsel?

An approach and some insights from one recent group looking at this case might be helpful.

I. *Who Is Responsible?*

A. Do your Guidelines for Responding help Susan Carr with her decision? Some people in the group felt that the most loving response was to offer clear advice to Ann based on her experience with other mothers; others felt that Susan's role was only to provide as much information as possible.

B. One person argued forcefully that this decision is not Susan Carr's at all. It's Ann's child, her term of pregnancy, her motherhood, and her family involved. Is what to do a matter for Ann Jones alone to decide?

C. Still another person was concerned about the rights of the father. "There needs to be an effort to locate and counsel with the father, to explain his rights and responsibilities whether marriage is coming or not." Do you agree with this opinion?

D. How can each of these people be most responsible to the baby? Would the child have greater possibilities to develop if Ann keeps the child and seeks to parent effectively, or is it better to let the child be given in adoption? Would social pressures affect the child in either decision? What aspects of the meaning of "responsibility" to the child should a person observe and consider?

This discussion led us to the issue of modeling.

II. *How Important Is Modeling?*

A. One person centered on the modeling necessary for the child's growth and said that Ann's decision depended on whether the child was a boy or a girl. "If it's a boy, then he will need a father particularly. If she is a girl, then a single woman can function just fine as a parent." What kind of models do you feel are the most significant for a growing child? How should this affect Ann's decision?

B. What kind of model does our response to Ann Jones offer to others? One person felt that Ann's dilemma was largely due to the increased societal acceptance of unwed persons living together. Thus acceptance of unwed mothers would be a further inroad to the open acceptance of loose and potentially destructive sexual standards. Acceptance of Ann Jones would offer our children a dangerous model. Is this approach consistent with your understanding of Christian living? Consider Jesus' statement to "judge not, that you be not judged" (Matt. 7:1). Does this apply in this instance?

C. The same group of adults began to remember the models and patterns of thought that surrounded them as they grew up. In those patterns selfishness on the mother's part in "unwed" situations was defined as keeping the baby. Was that true in the history of your own thought and theology in past times? Does such a "rule" make sense today in terms of logic and theology? Is there a way to change our images? Should we?

D. When Jesus asked Peter if he loved him, and Peter declared his devotion, Jesus responded, "Feed my lambs" (John 21:15–19). What would it mean to "feed" Ann Jones and her soon-to-be born child?

III. *What Are Ann's Resources?*

A. What social institutions provide places and systems of support for Ann Jones regardless of her decision?

B. Consider Susan's questions about Ann's family. How might the family help in either decision? Do you feel Ann needs this kind of support?

C. Is your own congregation a family that offers less judgment than help? What kind of inroads can you make to help your church group grow in acceptance and caring for members of your communion and for people in need of support?

IV. *Suggested Additional Reading*

Jesse Bernard, *The Future of Motherhood* (New York: Dial Press), 1974; Gail Sheehy, *Passages: Predictable Crises of Adult Life* (New York: E.P. Dutton), 1976.

6 / Matters of Life and Death: Guidelines for Hoping

Mary Gardner's Fourth Pregnancy

Vacation

Tom and Mary Gardner had planned their trip to Spain for more years than they could remember. They felt that at last their children, now twelve, eleven, and six, were old enough for them to be away for the four weeks. The children were all in school and Mary's mother, who had always been very close to the family, had flown up to "hold down the fort." Westminster Church, at which Tom had been a pastor for the past ten years, supported the leave with a monetary gift which made the trip possible and a farewell potluck supper.

As both Mary and Tom affirmed, the first week of the vacation was glorious. Thus when Mary began to experience nausea she was annoyed. Her chagrin turned to stunned confusion when she suddenly suspected she was pregnant. Several days later Mary shared her anxiety with Tom, stressing the element of there being no definite confirmation of her pregnancy.

Tom almost immediately suggested the possibility of an abortion, stating that through counseling with others and personal reflection he had come to see this as a theologically responsible option. Mary found her feeling of confidentiality turn to anger. She stated that she was confused, even deeply disappointed, but added that she didn't feel she could ever consider an abortion. Mary then added that they should wait until she had seen a doctor before they discussed it again.

When Mary left the large hospital in Barcelona with Tom, holding the "positive" medical report in her hand, she cried for nearly an hour. Tom comforted her and assured her that if she decided to have the baby that they would surely be able to manage and would love this child as deeply as the others. He stressed that his primary concern was for her.

During the next week, Mary became increasingly preoccupied with worrying about what she ought to do. She deeply respected Tom's judgment and tried to deal with his suggestion of an abortion. She remembered her pregnancy with Sara, who was so much younger than the other children and the real difficulty she had adjusting to Sara's arrival. Now with three children she felt that the quality of individual attention she considered essential for each child was already threatened by being spread too thin. And to be blatantly practical, Tom's salary covered the family needs only with careful budgeting. Another element was college education for three children, the first only a few years away. Furthermore, Mary had always wanted to support a child in a third world country through the church agency. She was sure this was a responsible use of family funds. Mary tried to pray about the decision on abortion but said she was really unable to find help here. Suddenly Mary declared to Tom that she should have an abortion while they were still in Spain and it would all be over with and no one at home would ever know.

Tom refused to consider this as an option, saying that they would be home in another week with a doctor they knew and trusted and that she might feel differently in her own home environment.

Return Home

When the Gardners returned to Elk City, Mary immediately made an appointment with her doctor. Tom went with her to the office. Dr. Weiss also confirmed the pregnancy, then clearly outlined the pregnancy termination procedure at what he felt was the best clinic in the area. However, when Mary began to discuss the abortion, she was unable to control her crying and expressed the great doubts she really had about the decision.

She had discussed with Dr. Weiss the possibility of sterilization following Sara's birth, but at the last moment did not request it. Dr. Weiss told Mary that if she decided to have this baby he would deliver it only on the condition that he perform a tubal ligation following the delivery. Upon Mary's insistence, he did make an appointment for her at the clinic the next week and filled out the necessary papers, but told her that she could always call him if she changed her mind.

Mary had consciously avoided her close friends after returning from the trip. Her depression deepened. Although she and Tom were able to discuss the decision to some extent, they both decided they needed the help of an uninvolved party. Mary called Carl Jenkins, an experienced family counselor who was also a good friend. He agreed to see them immediately.

Counseling

In the counseling situation, Mary was asked to express the uneasiness she was feeling.

"Well, Tom asked me way back in Barcelona if I had the choice, would I want to be pregnant. I definitely would not. We tried to prevent that from happening as best as we could. But now is the issue really what I *want?* How could God bless my consciously deciding to kill this new possibility of life growing in me? How can I believe that our other three children are beautiful, joyous gifts of God and that this one is just an accident?"

Mary continued, "I guess another thing that is bothering me terribly is that I know my family, certain friends, and surely some members of the church could never understand my having an abortion. The idea of sharing this with our children is absolutely unthinkable. I just could never tell any of them. As a child, any time I felt I had something to hide from my family, I always knew I was doing something wrong.

"And now I feel really abandoned. Tom wants this to be my decision, but I don't see how I can make it. I see so many valid reasons for not having this child, but I am unable to affirm that choice."

Carl Jenkins encouraged Tom to respond openly.

"I am pretty sensitive to the fact that Mary will sometimes look to me for answers. If I make this decision for her, then it becomes fully my responsibility. I'm very concerned about her choosing to have the abortion and then regretting it for the rest of her life. So I want to offer her love and support but not to make the decision for her."

"But," prodded Carl, "isn't it your decision too? Doesn't real support and respect for Mary demand that you tell her how *you* feel about the abortion?"

"Well, if I really speak on the gut level, I want Mary to have the abortion. We married right after college, and our first son was born a little less than a year later. For so many years she has been bound by her role in our home. I see a good part of this stemming from Mary's perception of herself as a responsible mother. In the past couple of years, though, as Sara has become more independent, I have been elated to watch Mary begin to find out who she really is, to begin some projects for herself, and, admittedly selfishly on my part, I rejoice in our having more time for one another. All that had begun to happen in the years before Sara's birth, and I felt at that time Mary's return to the full-time mother role was a real sacrifice for her and in many ways was destructive to her personal growth. I love her too much to want that to happen again."

With Carl's encouragement, Mary and Tom talked well into the evening about whether to have the abortion or not. When they rose to leave, Carl expressed his concern and love for them both and asked Mary, if she were willing, if she would call in a week to let him know what she decided.

Mary Gardner's Fourth Pregnancy
Study Guide

There are some situations in which a decision is demanded that do not fit into the context of the family or the church or the culture. The implications of the decision are broader than any of these single areas. They point to universal, human problems of life, sustenance, and death. We have described this as the "universal" context not because the specific problem applies to every individual in the world, but because the modeling impact in these decisions has a cumulative effect on the quality of human life in the world. The earlier cases were more domestic or internally focused. Those in this section focus on decisions about abortion, sustaining life, and death. In Christian living they point directly to creation, providence, and resurrection.

As a child develops, his or her awareness moves from total self-concern to those areas which influence value formation: the family, possibly the church, the culture in which one lives, and finally the wider context of universal concerns. The same is true of the modeling impact a person's decisions have on those around him or her. The primary impact may be on the self. Some decisions spread to the family. Still others to the church and the wider culture. Finally, a few decisions have, in a minor way, an impact on the universal questions of human existence that undergird all the other more standard decisions. Areas of one's personal growth and influence might be symbolized like this:

$$\text{Universal} \rightarrow \text{Culture} \rightarrow \text{Church} \rightarrow \text{Family} \rightarrow \text{Self}$$

As values are formed and decisions made in each of these areas of life, the Christian seeks responsible *guidelines* which will help one to evaluate the best response in a particular situation.

In addition to Love, Trust, and Responsibility, we now add the Christian guideline of Hope. Abundant life is clearly not possible without hope. The Christian is convinced that human existence has meaning because of what God has done for us in Jesus Christ. What we hope for will determine what we value, what we ask for, and how we act now. As we examine the cases in this section, we shall explore guidelines for hoping.

I. *Reasons for the Decision*

The discussion group might be asked to list the reasons for and against the decision to abort which confronts Mary and Tom Gardner. Note not only some of their possible feelings such as guilt, anger, frustration, duty, relief, etc., but also some of the factual concerns such as limited income; desire to support a "third world" child; restrictions on time, energy, and resources to develop parents' lives; responsibility of terminating potential human life; inability to share decision with family or congregation. There may be good personal, societal, and theological reasons cited for either decision. Realizing that *either* decision involves positive and negative elements, upon what criteria would one base a decision?

II. *Criteria for Judgment*

Abortion is a hotly disputed issue at the national and international level today. Both the laws of the land and the positions of the denominational churches make it clear that a decision to terminate a pregnancy should never be made lightly or in haste. Both the law and many church bodies agree that there are occasions when it may be morally justifiable. (A summary of the positions taken by many churches may be obtained from Religious Coalition for Abortion Rights, 100 Maryland Ave. N.E., Washington, D.C. 20002. Consult your local "Right to Life" organization for strong anti-abortion material.)

Some criteria questions may be: (1) When does life begin? Experts seem to be unable to agree on this question. (2) What does the Bible say? Most scholars agree that the Scriptures do not give specific guidance on the question of abortion. (3) What other criteria would be appropriate in the face of a conflict in interest between the mother and the fetus? Some persons have suggested that the issue is not simply one of mere physical existence of biological life, but rather the question of the quality of life. (4) What quality of life may be available to an unwanted child? Does putting the child up for adoption provide an adequate alternative? (5) Does the absolute opposition to abortion, and even more, contraception, have implications for the world population and hunger problems?

III. *Who Makes the Decision?*

Who has the primary responsibility for the decision? Is this Mary's decision because it is her body and she is most directly involved? Is it a decision to be made by Dr. Weiss on medical grounds? Do legal or theological positions demand a particular decision? Should Mary and Tom make the decision in a corporate way? Should they consult anyone besides Carl Jenkins, such as their parents, the children, members of the congregation, or others? Does the fact that this is the minister and his wife make a difference?

IV. *Signs of Hope*

Given a difficult and complex issue like abortion, what is it, if anything, that Mary and Tom can be hopeful about? What resources can Mary and Tom turn to in helping make the decision *and* in bearing the consequences of the decision either way it goes? Have they used all the appropriate resources to clarify the personal and moral issues? Who might help them with Mary's question about the difference between God's gift and "an accident"? Does responsible care and stewardship of the world mean that limitation must be put on the natural processes for the sake of ourselves, others, and the environment? Where could Tom and Mary realistically expect to find support and compassionate understanding for either decision? Mary is having a struggle with prayer. What might assist this avenue of grace to flow again? How would you apply to this case one of the strongest biblical affirmations of hope: "Nothing in all creation . . . can separate us from the love of God in Christ Jesus" (Romans 8:39 N.E.B.)? How might Christ's assurance of acceptance and forgiveness become a factor in this case? Some groups have found the guidelines for hope to involve:

> perseverance
> affirmation of God's good creation
> acceptance of Christ's grace/redemption
> assurance of forgiveness by God and neighbor.

V. *Use of the Case*

This case raises the issue of the meaning and quality of life, how priorities are decided, and how hope may allow us to get through a crisis in Christian Living. It would be appropriate for all forms of adult education, but particularly those that raise questions of the church's involvement in social issues. Women's associations and family groups may be especially interested in the focus on problem pregnancy.

VI. *Suggested Additional Reading*

James B. Nelson, *Human Medicine: Ethical Perspectives on New Medical Issues* (Minneapolis: Augsburg Press), 1973; C.S. Lewis, *The Great Divorce* (Riverside, N.J.: Macmillan), 1946, paperback.

Commitment for Larry Adams

Barbara and David Adams had just left pediatrician Ted Bailen's office with their two children, Larry, four years, and Tim, three weeks. With the arrival of the new baby the whole issue of whether or not to institutionalize Larry, a severely brain-damaged child, loomed bigger than ever. Tim gave all signs of being a healthy normal boy.

Dr. Bailen leaned back in his chair and tried mentally to gather the data he had acquired about the Adams over the past eight months. He had met them through the church in which Ted served as a deacon. Barbara and David had come to him looking for a pediatrician for Larry as well as seeking counseling in regard to a new baby.

In Ted Bailen's estimation Barbara and David Adams were a remarkable couple in a number of ways. They seemed open in their acceptance and love of Larry. They had both indicated that, in spite of the tremendous amount of time his care demanded, they could best express that love by not letting him determine their lives. Though both Barbara and David were active in their support of the special day school Larry attended, they were also involved in a diversity of community projects. Barbara was a church school teacher and a regular participant in a prison visitation program. David, a high school history teacher, had spent the past summer as a volunteer organizer for a farm worker's union, while Barbara supported the family with secretarial work. Just last year the Adams had moved to this small community of Hendersonville from Boston despite what they felt might be some limitations of living away from a large urban center. David had taken a job in the high school where he had found a particularly creative teaching program.

Ted Bailen remembered specifically the day eight months before when the Adams had first come to him. They were both excited as well as apprehensive about the coming of a second child. They had already taken Larry to a number of doctors for genetic counseling, trying to determine if his brain damage was purely accidental or if there was a strong likelihood that any other children might have similar problems. Ted recalled what the Adams had told him of Larry's medical history.

Larry Adams was born prematurely, weighing four pounds, with a cleft palate and widely spaced eyes. He was in an incubator and was over a month old before Barbara ever held him in her arms. A few days after Larry's birth, when Barbara was still in the hospital, she recounted that late one night she slipped down to the nursery section to look at her son. She stopped abruptly outside the door when she heard one of the nurses, who was feeding Larry, say to a co-worker, "Look at this messed up kid. Can you ever imagine him having sex with anything?" Barbara quietly returned to her room and said she was unable to mention the incident to anyone for many months.

Barbara had told Dr. Bailen, "I guess it was out of sympathy that no one said anything to us at first. Not even our parents talked about how Larry looked. I remember when we first had to face it. This was one Sunday morning after Larry, then three months old, had a seizure and we took him to the hospital. The doctor told us quite frankly that Larry was brain damaged, but he was very hesitant about giving us any prognosis. We were told that Larry *might* walk some day, and that by the time he was fifteen or sixteen he just *might* develop the abilities of a five-year-old. The doctor also said that many families with a child as severely damaged as Larry often decided to have the child institutionalized.

"I remember going to church later that morning. We sat in the balcony and I cried. I wasn't angry, but somehow I felt guilty. I didn't really grasp the whole situation but I was overwhelmed with how helpless that little baby was. I knew that we were taking care of someone very special. Then I didn't know what I was crying for. Now I do. I still cry when I realize that when Larry is sixteen or seventeen years old, he won't even be able to take care of himself."

David added that his greatest feeling at the time was disappointment. "I had had all of these ideas about my first child— all the things we were going to do together. Now that I look back, we were also having to deal with this nonsense about Larry being punished for some other life or that somehow *we* were being punished."

In thinking about the months that followed, Barbara had

said that one of the frustrating things for her was Larry's weight. "I'd go to the pediatrician's office and see all of those fat and healthy children; I knew Larry wasn't gaining. Whether it was logical or not, I felt terribly responsible and guilty about this. I believe that the acceptance and support of friends was as important to me then as it has ever been."

Barbara remembered that this was particularly true of a group of nursing mothers she had joined. She had been determined to breast feed her child. During the many weeks Larry was in the hospital, she expressed her milk for him. Barbara told Dr. Bailen that at this time and during the difficult first months to follow she was especially appreciative of the loving concern of these mothers.

Dr. Bailen recalled that it was during these first months that the Adams said their sense of responsibility for Larry was heightened. The baby was frequently subject to seizures and several times spent days in the hospital and came quite close to dying. The concerted efforts of a medical team helped him pull through.

Barbara and David said that at this time they were aware of gentle messages from both sets of grandparents to consider putting Larry in an institution. This was the first grandchild in both families. David recalled, "My father is one of the most gentle and kind people I know, but I think Larry wasn't really a person to my parents. I resented their feelings at first, but now I realize that their primary concern was for us. They didn't want Larry to become a burden that could destroy our marriage or disrupt our lives as I know has happened in some cases. At first I think Barbara and I were both threatened by our parents' concern. But at the time we were able to express a desire to raise Larry as best we could. Somehow an institution was the easy way out. We incorporated Larry into our lifestyle and took him with us wherever we went. It was more important than ever for us to keep him and protect him. Again the acceptance of our friends was incredibly important. We had a marvelous first birthday party for Larry and invited our parents as well as a number of friends. Larry had seizures all during the party."

Larry had progressed slowly. Now at age four he weighed twenty-five pounds. Barbara said that his vacant stare no longer bothered her and that Larry was beginning to respond to her voice, grasp toys, and even crawl around. Barbara had added, "Larry lost weight when I tried to get him to feed himself, but he is able to hold a cup now."

David and Barbara said that for about two years they had only talked "academically" about whether or not they would or could have other children. Then after a third year they definitely decided they wanted another child and began the rounds of genetic counseling, being referred to different pediatricians who examined Larry. Barbara recalled that the most disturbing visit they had was with a doctor who "examined Larry like a bunch of grapes" and then insisted that he be put in an institution. He said there was a good chance that a second child would be normal and that Larry would not only demand more of his mother's time than was healthy but he would have a retarding effect on any brothers and sisters. He advised the Adams to begin immediately the process of putting Larry on a waiting list for one of the state facilities. Barbara had later told Dr. Bailen, "This was another crying day. I almost believed him. He was so very clear and firm. But we didn't *want* to do it."

A month later when Barbara learned she was pregnant, the Adams had come to Ted Bailen. Dr. Bailen recalled the information he had given the Adams on their first visit. He tried to help them get a clear picture about the life of a child in a state institution. He said Larry would have food, shelter, and clothing but that he would not have the same kind of care and support as at home. He stated that a crucial element was their commitment as parents. They had to be realistic about that and they must also look to the future. In past years brain-damaged children were so susceptible to infection that they often died in infancy. This was not true today. The number of seizures Larry had were less frequent all the time; he could live for many years.

In his office a few minutes before, Ted Bailen had seen Larry grab at the baby's head and watched Barbara gently take his hand away. Dr. Bailen knew this had to be the Adams' decision—not his. But they had come to him for advice. As a doctor he saw no clear-cut medical guidelines. Ted Bailen pondered, "As a fellow Christian, how can I help Barbara and David evaluate the priorities involved in this decision for Larry and Tim as well as for themselves?"

Commitment for Larry Adams
Study Guide

"We know that in everything God works for good with those who love him" (Romans 8:28). Faith in God's love for us is central to a Christian's *hope* in the midst of hardship. In turn as we seek to love God, we try to follow Christ's commandment to love and care for others. However, in cases such as this about Larry Adams, we are often unclear about the most loving way to care for those in need. Is the most loving response to the entire Adams family to place Larry in a state institution, or is loving an issue of increased commitment to the care of Larry at home?

I. *Implications of Commitment*

A. One possible way to begin discussion might be to ask for an immediate vote on the case: Should the Adams institutionalize Larry or not? Then follow this with a period of analysis as to *why* each person voted as she or he did. Responses could be listed in separate categories; for either the "yes" or "no" vote there are objective reasons (Barbara's time, Tim's well-being, etc.) as well as feeling reasons (guilt, anger, relief, etc.).

    1. The decision to care for Larry at home might involve:

    (a) A greater commitment of time and emotional energy for Barbara. What are the feelings involved in her desire to protect Larry? What is the foundation for these feelings?

    (b) The effect on Tim. (Note: Many pediatricians and psychologists would disagree with the thesis that Larry would necessarily have a "retarding effect" on Tim.) Would Tim get less attention from his parents if Larry is at home? Where would Tim find models for new skills?

(c) How David feels about the decision. Why do you think David reacted to his parents as he did? How may David's "disappointment" in Larry affect his feelings now?

2. Consider the issues involved in the decision to institutionalize Larry. What would be the advantages and disadvantages of this decision? What feelings are involved? How important is guilt in this option?

II. *What It Means to Be Human*

A. In your discussion of David and Barbara Adams' feelings about Larry, members of the group may have noted that both parents mention their concern for Larry's acceptance. At this point, consider discussing what it means to be human and to be made in "the image of God" (Gen. 1:27). You might list the criteria on the board. Does being fully human refer to physical or mental development, to one's responsiveness? Is someone who has limited capabilities "less than human"? Does being fully human mean the freedom to develop whatever capacities you have been given?

Would it have been more loving to allow Larry to die as an infant? What does your answer reveal about your understanding of human life? Does the degree of one's handicap affect your response?

What are the implications of the hospital nurse's comment about Larry? Why do you think Barbara resented the doctor who examined Larry like a "bunch of grapes"? Why do you think it is often difficult for many of us fully to accept those with physical or mental handicaps? How would you explain the guilt which both David and Barbara express?

B. Is Larry Adams a responsibility of the extended Christian family, or is he the responsibility of Barbara and David alone? Why or why not? There is an enormous expense to taxpayers for the provision of full time institutional care. Is this fair? Do you feel the same way about those who are economically handicapped? Why or why not? (Your group might consider researching the community and state facilities for those who are physically, mentally, or economically handicapped.

Why would this or would it not be an area with which the church has specific concerns?)

III. *What It Means to Hope*

Millions of people in the world suffer from lifelong disabilities. Christ declared that he came so that we may have life and "have it abundantly" (John 10:10). Does this mean that those who suffer with an affliction are being punished or are removed from God's love? What might abundant life mean for the Adams? With either decision how does the family keep alive hope for themselves and for Larry? How might Christ's promise of forgiveness free them to make a responsible decision?

In this case there is a tension between hoping for oneself and hoping for others. There seems to be no medical evidence that Larry will physically or mentally improve. Following the Guidelines for Hoping, what do you hope for in this case? Does loving and caring for Larry involve hoping he may become more capable?

IV. *Resources of Grace*

How can Ted Bailen respond with hope and love? It is clear that Barbara and David's friends have been sources of loving support in the past. How might they help now? Consider the kind of support the Adams need whichever decision they make. What is the importance of prayer and forgiveness in this case? To what resources in the church or the community could Ted Bailen turn? Are there others who may have dealt with this same kind of decision?

V. *Suggested Additional Reading*

Milton Mayeroff, *On Caring* (New York: Harper & Row), 1972, paperback; C.F.D. Moule, *The Meaning of Hope* (Philadelphia: Fortress Press), 1963, paperback; and *The Exceptional Parent*, a magazine designed from the point of view of the parents of handicapped children. Order from 262 Beacon St., Boston, Mass. 02116, or 8823 Santa Fe Lane, Overland Park, Kansas 66212. See especially: Maxine Green, "Loving a Special Child" (June, 1975), pp. 9–15, and "Let Us All Stop Blaming the Parents," editorial (August-September, 1971), pp. 3–5.

The Death of Fanny Grimes

When Rick Noble had to go into the city on business, he determined to stop and see Fanny Grimes at the hospital. She had been there off and on for the past two years. Rick wasn't comfortable about visiting in the hospital, but he supposed few people from Lynn got into town who would go by to see her. The Grimes lived on the outskirts of Lynn, and they also stayed on the edge of the congregation. Fanny and George had always been kind of independent folk; and while Rick had known them over a long period of time, he did not see them often. The Grimes had owned a hardware store in Lynn, and George still worked for Lonnie Beane, who bought him out five years ago. Since Fanny's illness, though, George worked only on Wednesdays and Saturdays. He was almost fully retired, probably sixty-five or so. Fanny must have been a couple of years younger.

After he made the business calls, Rick Noble parked and asked at the information for her room number—502. Fanny looked pale, with machines and tubes, medicines and charts around her. She still greeted him with the usual, "Rick Noble! How's the family?" Rick tried to focus attention on her face, to pretend not noticing all the things in the room. "Fine. Gladys wanted to come with me, but I had some business to do. We're all fine. How are you feeling?"

"Oh, all right. Little dull pain here and there. They take good care of me here, though."

"Same kidney acting up?" asked Rick.

"I think it's worse than normal. They say some fluid gets around in my body and makes me feel worse than I have been. Did you see George outside?"

"No, I didn't," Rick said. "Is he staying in town?"

A nurse whisked in, apologized for the interruption and asked Rick to step outside a few minutes. "Is he one of your sons?" she said to Fanny.

"No, he's a friend from Lynn, member of our church."

"I'll see you, Fanny. I'd better get on home." Rick said as he retreated toward the door.

"I wish you'd see George a minute if you can spare the

time," she called as he backed out. "And thanks for taking the time to come by."

"I sure hope you feel better soon." Rick waved goodbye. "I will look and see if he's outside."

George was sitting in the waiting room. Rick greeted him. "George, hi. I had to be in town anyhow, and I've been wanting to see you."

George motioned Rick to a chair. "Things aren't going so well."

"Fanny doesn't look good. . . . All that equipment and the tubes don't help." Rick said.

"That's the dialysis machine. We have one at home. It's never even been used. I bought it for $9,500 just last month. It takes the fluid out of her body, and they said we needed one. Then this. . . ." George's voice trailed off.

"What? It didn't work?"

"I don't know. Never got to see. I called the City Equipment Company and they won't even buy it back. No, she just took a turn for the worse, and they said she better stay awhile here. Now Dr. Knowland says the fluid has gotten in her lungs, and she'll just have to stay here as long as she keeps breathing. He uses all kinds of fancy words, but it amounts to my decision. Do I take her home to die, or do I keep her here and let her just die slowly . . . maybe next week or maybe next month?" George lit one cigarette from another.

"If I take her home, it'll all be on me. It'll be quick and pretty sure to happen in a few days. If she stays here, the hospital will be taking care of her. She's got the pain, and it won't get any better in that department."

Rick offered George a cup of coffee. They found a little room next to the instant coffee dispenser.

"Fanny and I have been married almost thirty-five years— it'll be that on March 21st. These last years have really been hard ones. You know she's been pretty sick for almost three years. Every two weeks, then every week, I had to bring her in to see Dr. Knowland. That was when things were going good. At bad times she had to stay here. . . ."

"The nurse mentioned a son. I didn't know you had chil-

dren." Rick ventured, and he had known the Grimes a long
time.

"Yes, Tom and Bill. . . . two boys . . . but they've been gone
a long time now. Tom and his family live in Utah, a long piece
from here. Bill never married. He works for Uncle Sam. We
haven't seen either one for years. Tom writes every so often, or
his wife Hazel does. Bill just sends us something every Christmas. You know, since we've been together—Fanny and me—
every Christmas has been special. We took our trips after that
buying rush. Told everybody we were doing inventory. Went
all the way to the Gulf coast one year. Now this . . . What should
I do? Take her on home? Leave her here?"

"What do the doctors advise, George?" Rick stole a glance
at his watch.

"They won't tell me. They say it's up to me. That machine
at home won't help now, though. It's never even been used!
And the company won't take it back. How do you like that? If
I take her home, she'll die quick. If she stays here it won't
change much. Just take longer, probably. I sure wish somebody
would just come out and tell me one way or the other. What
would you do if it was Gladys?"

"I don't know, George. I really don't."

"It wouldn't be so bad if there was some chance of her
getting better. I don't know even if they've told her how bad
it is. She acts like we will be going home soon, like the times
before. Now it won't help, though. Should I tell her?"

"George, you have been really close for a long time. You
must know best what to do."

"It's a lot on my mind. I never had to make a choice like
this before. Wish I had somebody to share it with. Doctors use
fancy words, but I just know it amounts to my decision. What
should I do?"

The Death of Fanny Grimes
Study Guide

The final case in the collection focuses on death and dying,
but it also brings into consideration the doctrines of resurrec-

tion and immortality. "Concerning those who are asleep," Paul tells us we should "not grieve as others do who have no hope" (1 Thess. 4:13). This hope centers on faith in God's promise of resurrection and of God's continuing love. For a Christian, it is in the face of death that the concept of hope can become a real force in the manner in which one actually lives.

In Christian history the meaning of death and life after death often have been neglected. In our own time, with natural death processes obscured by life-support systems of various sorts, we have a greater responsibility for ethical and religious choices regarding the "where," "when," and "how" of death. Medical personnel and others in society are increasingly concerned with these "final" questions about human life. Who decides in matters of life-support systems? What are the various responsibilities of those in grief, and how can they, as well as the dying person, be assisted? How might the guidelines for hoping provide a connection between the New Testament promise of resurrection and our concern with death?

I. *Stages of Dying*

Perhaps the best known American authority on death and dying, Elisabeth Kübler-Ross, isolated and described various "stages" she discovered among dying persons. These stages are quite complex and interactive (not usually mere successions of attitudes and actions). She did not find that her schema applied in all cases. But naming the stages and understanding that death and dying is a process remains important. The stages in the process as she discovered them are:

A. *Denial and Isolation.* Denial occurs both initially in the "This can't be about me!" expletives and the recurrent denial from time to time in the whole process. Kübler-Ross emphasizes the healthiness of this denial stage: "Denial functions as a buffer after unexpected shocking news, allows the patient to collect himself, and, with time, mobilize other, less radical defenses." A portion of this stage also involves one's desire to cut off relationships, to isolate oneself from hospital staff and personal support systems.

B. *Anger.* "This anger is displaced in all directions and

projected onto the environment at times almost at random."
Hostility toward "incompetent" doctors, "inadequate" tests, an
"unloving" family, "bad" food, etc. Kübler-Ross says the patient
is yelling, "I am alive, don't forget that. You can hear my voice,
I am not dead yet!"

C. *Bargaining.* Little victories are sought and wallowed in.
One more time for. . . . It is "really an attempt to postpone,"
according to her. "It has to include a prize offered 'for good
behavior,' it also sets a self-imposed 'deadline,' . . . and it includes an implicit promise that the patient will not ask for more
if this one postponement is granted." Most bargains are with
God, personally unvoiced and in fact hidden from others.

D. *Depression.* "His numbness or stoicism, his anger and
rage will soon be replaced with a great sense of loss." The
burdens of financial cost, personal disfigurement, and dashed
hopes are but some of the causes which naturally accompany
the process.

E. *Acceptance.* Gradually increasing sleep-times, unwill-
ingness to bother about the rest of the world, and other external
evidences correspond to an inner change on the part of people
who move through the other stages before death actually occurs. As Dr. Kübler-Ross states, though, this should not be confused with a "time of happy resignation." Rather it is a sense of
unfeeling and "a rest before the journey." [From Elisabeth
Kübler-Ross, *On Death and Dying* (New York: Macmillan,
1969). Her most recent work has focused on the "life-after-
death" experiences of people. She firmly believes in personal
immortality. See Elisabeth Kübler-Ross, editor, *Death: The
Final Stage of Growth,* (Englewood Cliffs, N.J.: Prentice-Hall,
1975.)]

II. *Identifying the Death Process*

If you decide to refer to the "stages" of Kübler-Ross, the
discussion leader might ask for any clarification of additions to
the stages that seem necessary. In this particular case what
evidence is there for determining where Fanny "is" in the
death process? You realize that both the descriptions of the

"stages" of dying and those of the Grimes are extremely brief, and your conclusions will be very tentative. How does this analysis help you to understand Fanny and George's situation? How might Fanny be helped to face her own death? Do you think she already knows? What kind of hope is possible for Fanny? What can George hope for?

III. *Responsibility for the Decision*

Whether or not you included discussion of the dying process, some considerations that have grown out of past discussions might be pertinent for your group also.

A. Whose decision is it to do anything at this point? Fanny, George, the two of them together? Do all persons have the right to share in the decision about their death if the circumstances are similar to those in the case? Do all want to?

B. Has communication broken down between George and Fanny? If so, how can it be restored? If not, what is the nature of George's indecision?

C. What are Rick Noble's alternatives right now, and what should he do? What resources of grace can he call upon? How could he share hope with Fanny and George?

D. Where is the church, the extended family, in this situation? How might the church minister to Fanny, George, their sons?

E. What is the relationship of the medical personnel to the Grimes in this case? What should it be?

IV. *Summary of Learning*

This case, as many others in this collection, can provide a "springboard" to deeper study on issues and needs that are exposed by the case discussion. Many groups have found a brief book entitled *Good Grief* by Granger Westberg (Philadelphia: Fortress Press, 1976) to be an excellent resource for either preparation or followup on the grief process.

You may also wish to move toward discussion of "learnings" from this case. For those who have used a series of cases, this case may be a helpful instrument for reviewing the Guidelines for Loving, Trusting, Responding, and Hoping developed by your discussion group. All are applicable to this case. The summary would serve as a review of the biblical guidelines and resources of grace suggested in previous chapters, but, more importantly, could reflect the communal insights and faith of your own group.

V. *Suggested Additional Reading*

Elisabeth Kübler-Ross, *On Death and Dying* (New York: The Macmillan Co.), 1970; and Marjorie C. McCoy, *To Die With Style* (Nashville: Abingdon), 1974.

Appendix: Notes on Historical Background and Additional Resources for the Case Method

The introductory essays suggest the link between the Bible and the case method of teaching. In the process of learning it is the application of biblical insights and the wisdom of the faith community to actual experiences which helps the material "come alive." The learner becomes a participant and not an observer.

In secular education in the U.S., case study began during the late 1800s. Christopher C. Langdell was appointed Dean of Harvard Law School in 1870 by President Charles Eliot. Langdell determined that decisions of courts should become primary data for legal education. He thought this use of legal cases would best teach a doctrine "by studying the cases in which it is embodied." Protests came from faculty and students, and for a whole decade the use of cases was questioned more than accepted at Harvard Law School.

Schools of social work as well as other law schools began using cases. Medical schools, also developing their use of cases, offered a different perspective in professional education. In 1908 Harvard Business School began with a case-centered approach to business administration.

In several different areas, attempts to use the case method in theological education were already under way when the Case-Study Institute opened in 1971 with a grant from the Sealantic Fund, Inc. The Institute was specifically formed to test and teach the application of the case approach to theological education. During the successive summers in which a CSI Summer Workshop has been conducted, more than 150 professors from seminaries across the continent have been initiated in case teaching methods. They used the Harvard Business School model initially, but most have also come to use other related forms of the case method.

How to Order Additional Cases

These professors, participants in the Case-Study Institute, have been responsible for the writing of more than 300 actual cases, some only one page long and others the size of a small book. All of these cases are copyrighted by number and are available to institutions and church groups virtually at cost. The cases are listed in a bibliography provided by the agency which distributes them: The Intercollegiate Case Clearing House (ICCH), Soldiers Field, Boston, Mass. 02163. An ICCH Bibliography of *Cases for Theological Education* (1977), compiled by Louis Weeks, provides brief descriptions of each case plus relevant data of author, location, time, and issues considered. Some teaching guides are available for these cases. Additional cases may provide resources for class discussion or for a particular theme or issue not considered in this volume.

Three books employing cases which may also be of help to the reader are: Keith R. Bridston, Fred K. Foulkes, Ann D. Myers, and Louis Weeks, eds., *Case Book on Church and Society* (Nashville: Abingdon Press), 1974; Robert A. Evans and Thomas D. Parker, eds., *Christian Theology: A Case Method Approach* (New York: Harper & Row), 1976; and Jack Rogers, Ross MacKenzie, and Louis Weeks, *Case Studies in Christ and Salvation* (Philadelphia: The Westminster Press), 1977.